SpringerBriefs in Computer Science

Series Editors
Stan Zdonik
Peng Ning
Shashi Shekhar
Jonathan Katz
Xindong Wu
Lakhmi C. Jain
David Padua
Xuemin Shen
Borko Furht

For further volumes:
http://www.springer.com/series/10028

Thomas Plötz · Gernot A. Fink

Markov Models for Handwriting Recognition

Dr. Thomas Plötz
Culture Lab
School of Computing Science
Newcastle University
Grand Assembly Rooms, King's Walk
Newcastle upon Tyne
NE1 7RU
UK
e-mail: thomas.ploetz@newcastle.ac.uk

Prof. Dr. Gernot A. Fink
Department of Computer Science
Technische Universität Dortmund
Otto-Hahn-Strasse 16
44227 Dortmund
Germany
e-mail: Gernot.Fink@udo.edu

ISSN 2191-5768
ISBN 978-1-4471-2187-9
DOI 10.1007/978-1-4471-2188-6
Springer London Dordrecht Heidelberg New York

e-ISSN 2191-5776
e-ISBN 978-1-4471-2188-6

British Library Cataloguing in Publication Data
A catalogue record for this book is available from the British Library

Cover design: eStudio Calamar, Berlin/Figueres

Printed on acid-free paper

Springer is part of Springer Science+Business Media (www.springer.com)

Preface

The history of the development of Markov model-based pattern recognition methods is closely related to the field of automatic speech recognition. There, hidden Markov models and related techniques were developed from their infancy into a mature framework for the analysis of sequential data. Not before the 1990s researchers who were working on speech recognition before transferred the technology to the field of optical character recognition with a special focus on handwritten script.

In much the same way the authors of this book made their way from spoken language technology to handwriting recognition research. It started with a project lead by Gernot A. Fink and Gerhard Sagerer at Bielefeld University, Germany, which focussed on camera-based handwriting recognition and first addressed the task of reading handwritten notes on a whiteboard. This research initiative resulted in a successor project lead by the authors at TU Dortmund, Germany, which aimed at a more thorough investigation of the problem of camera-based whiteboard reading.

In the context of these research projects the authors' expertise in the field developed, leading to a first successful tutorial on "Markov Models for Handwriting Recognition" presented at the International Conference on Document Analysis and Recognition (ICDAR) in 2007 [1]. Based on this tutorial, a survey article on the use of Markov models of offline handwriting recognition followed that appeared in the International Journal on Document Analysis and Recognition (IJDAR) in 2009 [2]. This article formed the basis of the material presented in this book. The treatment of Markov model-based techniques was thoroughly revised and extended in order to cover both online and offline recognition approaches.

Over the years the authors' research in handwriting recognition significantly benefitted from the availability of datasets collected by Horst Bunke and his group at University of Bern, Switzerland. Therefore, we would like to express our sincere thanks to Horst Bunke for providing this valuable resource—including some samples used for illustrations in this book—without which our own and many other people's research in handwriting recognition would not have been possible.

References

1. Fink GA, Plötz T (2007) Tutorial on Markov models for handwriting recognition. In: Proceedings of international conference on document analysis and recognition, Curitiba, Brazil
2. Plötz T, Fink GA (2009) Markov models for offline handwriting recognition: a survey. Int J Doc Anal Recognit 12(4):269–298

Newcastle and Dortmund, July 2011   Thomas Plötz
                                                                           Gernot A. Fink

Contents

Chapter 1
Introduction

Abstract Reading systems, i.e., machines that try to recreate the human capabilities of reading printed or handwritten script, are of fundamental scientific and commercial interest. They play a major role in a number of application domains including, for example, document analysis (mail sorting, bank check processing, archiving), and innovative human-computer interfaces (pen based input). Similar to, for example, spoken language, handwritten script corresponds to sequential data, which requires specialized analysis techniques that can cope with segmentation and classification in a reasonable manner. Markov models represent a well suited framework for the analysis of sequential data in general, and for processing handwritten script in particular. Already introduced about a century ago, in the last few decades they gained popularity also for handwriting recognition. Especially hidden Markov models in combination with Markov chain—i.e., n-gram—models have been employed very successfully for a number of applications of both online and offline handwriting recognition. This book gives an overview of theoretical concepts as well as practical aspects of Markov model based handwriting recognition.

Keywords Reading systems · Handwriting recognition · Online vs. offline recognition · Document analysis · Hidden Markov model · HMM · n-gram language model · History · Applications

A major goal of pattern recognition research is to recreate human perception capabilities in artificial systems. As a special aspect of visual perception the ability to read machine-printed or handwritten text is one such remarkable ability of humans that is—even today—hardly matched by machine intelligence. Since the very first efforts to achieve optical character recognition (OCR), i.e., to automatically read machine-printed texts, the research field dealing with artificial reading systems has undergone significant changes in methodology and made substantial progress towards its ultimate goal.

For example, the problem of reading machine-printed addresses in a mail-sorting machine—especially with the impressive speed of the commercial systems

T. Plötz and G. A. Fink, *Markov Models for Handwriting Recognition*,
SpringerBriefs in Computer Science, DOI: 10.1007/978-1-4471-2188-6_1,
© Thomas Plötz 2011

available—can be considered solved. The availability of more general commercial solutions for OCR demonstrates that the technology is quite mature in this field already. However, as soon as the variability in the script to be read becomes more prominent, as it is the case for degraded documents or—even more severely—for handwritten text, current technology reaches its limits. Consequently, the task of automatically reading handwriting with close-to-human performance is still an open problem and the central issue of an active field of research.

In almost all endeavors to build artificial perception systems, research focuses on methods that automatically learn from sample data. For learning models of sequential data—as text can be considered to be with some approximation—approaches based on Markovian models proved very successful, especially in the field of automatic speech recognition. Today, systems based on Markov models (MM) can also be considered the state-of-the-art for automatic handwriting recognition (HWR). Since their first introduction into the field almost two decades ago, considerable progress has been made in adapting MM-based techniques to this new domain. However, in contrast to the field of automatic speech recognition, where quasi standard procedures are established, researchers are still exploring a wide range of possibilities in applying MM-based methods to the challenging problem of reading handwritten text.

The goal of this book is to provide a comprehensive overview of the application of Markov models in the research field of handwriting recognition. The term "Markov model" here refers to both the widely used hidden Markov models (HMMs) and the less complex Markov-chain models. To some limited extent general foundations of automatic HWR not explicitly related to the application of Markov models will be discussed here as well. However, for more detailed treatments of this general state-of-the-art the reader is referred to the broader surveys, which have been published in recent years (e.g., [1–5]).

Techniques for automatic handwriting recognition can be distinguished as being either online or offline, depending on the particular processing strategy applied. Online recognition is performed as the text to be recognized is written. Therefore, the process of handwriting has to be captured online, e.g., using some pressure sensitive devices. They provide rich sequences of sensor data including geometrical positions of the stylus as well as temporal information about the writing process, which is *the* big advantage of online approaches. In contrast, offline recognition is performed after the text has been written. For this purpose, images of the handwriting are processed, which are captured, e.g., using a scanner or a camera.

It is commonly agreed that online handwriting recognition corresponds to the easier of the two principle problems. Consequently, at least for certain application domains like pen-based input interfaces substantial progress has been achieved. In fact, commercially available products suggest that the problem of online HWR can be considered as being close to solved (cf., e.g., [6]). Actually, one of the most successful online handwriting recognizers (Microsoft's system for tablet and desktop computer operating systems [6]), is in-fact based on an alternative, non-Markovian modeling approach, namely time-delay neural networks.[1] It is the success and the effectiveness of such online handwriting recognizers that has freed resources to move towards much more complicated tasks like, e.g., online sketch recognition (cf., e.g., [9] for a very impressing physics simulator). Current research in online handwriting recognition, therefore, focuses on more challenging scripts as, for example, Arabic (cf., e.g., [10]), the group of Indic scripts (cf., e.g., [11]), and the non-alphabetic scripts used for writing Japanese (cf. [12]) and Chinese (cf. [13]).

The fundamentals of Markovian modeling for handwriting recognition are similar for both online and offline procedures. Given a sequential stream of input data, either obtained directly from the sensor as in the online case or artificially serialized as for offline recognition, a two-stage stochastic process is used to model both the appearance and the structure of handwriting. By means of efficient and robust training and decoding algorithms, Markov model based recognition systems can effectively be realized for classification systems at large scales. This book provides a comprehensive description of the general architecture of such recognition systems along with detailed explanations of the underlying theory of Markovian models. In contrast to comparable treatments of these topics in the literature we not only cover the majority of current research on Markov-model based handwriting recognition but also concentrate on practical aspects of offline handwriting recognition systems.

Although HWR shows parallels to classical optical character recognition (OCR), i.e., the analysis of machine printed text, the scope of this book is focused on handwriting recognition. If not absolutely necessary, we do not cover specialties of OCR applications. The recognition of handwriting data is addressed, which exhibits *unconstrained* writing style in mainly Roman or Arabic scripts.[2] More precisely, the recognition of non-alphabetic scripts (like Kanji) is not covered. Reasonable exceptions, where certain substantial similarities to alphabetic scripts recognition exist, will be discussed though.

1.1 History

The application of Markov models has a fairly long history in various domains. At the beginning of the past century the Russian mathematician Andrej Andrejewitsch Markov first applied such a type of statistical model for the analysis of character sequences [15]. Honoring his fundamental developments, statistical models that share the same basic properties were named after Markov.

The basic technology of hidden Markov models—the most prominent variant of Markov models—was originally used for speech recognition applications.

---

[1] Time-delay neural networks (TDNNs) were proposed for automatic speech recognition in [7] and first applied to an online handwriting recognition task in [8].

[2] Interestingly techniques for the recognition of Latin and Arabic script are more similar than one might expect when only visually comparing documents written in, e.g., English or an Arabic language [14].

Fundamental developments in the late 1960s started to allow the robust and efficient automatic analysis of time-dependent signal data for real life scenarios (cf., e.g., [16–18]). After substantial research efforts Markovian models can today be considered the state-of-the-art technology in the area of automatic speech recognition (cf., e.g., [19]). In the last 20+ years this concept has also been transferred to the domain of handwriting recognition

Markov models are used for both online and offline handwriting recognition. Especially relevant for the latter, the application of the sliding window principle can be understood as one of the most important historic 'milestones' for successful Markov-model based handwriting recognition [20, 21]. Its application allows for the effective serialization of handwriting data, which can be considered as *the* prerequisite for the successful application of Markov models for offline recognition.

During the last few years research w.r.t. Markov-model based handwriting recognition has made substantial progress. Comparable to their application in the speech recognition domain, certain procedures have been established now serving as quasi standard for offline HWR based on Markov models. Just to mention two examples practically all current recognizers are derived by applying (variants of) Baum-Welch training on sample data (see Sect. 3.3.1 for details) resulting in most cases in (semi-) continuous output models. They are usually based on Gaussian mixture densities. Furthermore, and again similar to speech processing, the integration of Markov-chain models into HWR systems is very promising. According to recent publications, combined recognizers integrating both HMMs as script appearance models and statistical *n*-grams as language models represent one of the latest trends in handwriting recognition (cf., e.g., [4, 22]).

1.2 Applications

Markov-model based approaches are today widely used in the application field of automatic HWR. In addition to their use in academic research, they also play an important role in commercial applications in industrial contexts.

Online handwriting recognition has its main application field in human-computer interaction, more specifically for intuitive input mechanisms. Prominent examples are Personal Digital Assistants (PDA) or stylus-based tablet computers (cf. [6] for an excellent overview of pen-based computing). Probabilistic modeling techniques, such as Markovian models, are applied for efficient decoding of either isolated characters (as in the pioneering Palm^{TM} PDA devices), or complete words and short sentences (as in tablets). Although certain publications regarding Markov-model based recognition of isolated characters exist (for offline recognizers cf., e.g., [23–26]), it is rather doubtful whether the use of these models is appropriate for this kind of data. Instead, the approach shows its strength especially for cursive script, i.e., character sequences written in a more or less connected style. Thus, at least words should be considered in order to benefit from the properties of Markov models. The actual recognition is either performed for isolated words or for connected words.

The latter is the more complicated but the more realistic use case since, for example, full sentences can be treated without relying on prior—successful—segmentation. Consequently, actual document analysis based on text recognition becomes possible.

Markovian models have also been applied very successfully to online handwriting recognition on whiteboards [27]. Hereby either the whiteboard itself serves as sensor for data recording or the pen used for writing. In the former case the board, i.e., a pressure sensitive surface, itself tracks the movements of the pen (or the finger). As of today this technology can be found, for example, in every classroom in the UK. A number of commercial suppliers of such so-called smart or interactive whiteboards exists including, for example, Promethean^{TM} or Smart^{TM}. In the latter case the pen itself is tracked by some sensor system, e.g., utilizing ultrasonic or infra-red technology as for the e-beam^{TM} system. Our own research even suggests [28–31] that it might be possible in the future to read unconstrained whiteboard content without the need for special pen-tracking hardware only by using a camera.

Another important application domain for online handwriting recognition is signature verification as it is, for example, widely used for authorization purposes in legal transactions (e.g., parcel delivery, credit or debit card payment). By analyzing the signature online—in contrast to taking a picture of the final signature and applying offline recognition procedures—also the dynamics of the writing process are taken into account. In addition to its final appearance, the way people write their signature is very idiosyncratic. Hence, it can be used for biometric analysis as it is required for writer identification. Markovian models traditionally play an important role in online signature verification reasoned by their capabilities of capturing the dynamics of sequential data (cf., e.g., [32] or [33]).

Compared to the rather well-defined domain of online handwriting recognition, a larger variety of offline applications using Markovian models exists. Most related systems have been developed for the automatization of processing larger amounts of documents. Postal automation thereby represents the certainly most prominent domain, i.e., address reading, e.g., for mail sorting. In recent years tremendous efforts have been directed towards this issue (cf., e.g., [34–37]). They have resulted in powerful recognition systems, which are successfully applied by major postal service companies (cf., e.g., [3, 38, 39]).

Markov-model based handwriting recognition is furthermore applied to the automatic processing of bank checks and official forms as regularly considered by insurance companies, banks, governmental organizations etc. Various recognizers for different languages have been developed and are applied (cf., e.g., [40, 41]). Automatic check processing requires digit recognition (with the special case of analyzing touching digits) and offline signature verification (cf., e.g., [42–44]).

Markov models have also been used for explicit segmentation of handwritten texts at word level [45, 46], and for layout analysis of complete documents (cf., e.g., [47–49]).

1.3 Structure

The remainder of the book is organized as follows. In the next chapter we will first give a qualitative overview of the architecture of a typical HWR system based on Markov models. Key references will be given for only those aspects that are not integral parts of an MM-based system and will be treated in more detail in subsequent sections. The concepts and algorithms behind the MM-based recognition paradigm will then be presented in Chap. 3. Subsequently, in Chap. 4 we will review the different methods applied and solutions proposed for solving the key problems in MM-based HWR systems. Markov-model based handwriting recognition has already become a mature research field with important applications in both academic and industrial context. For these purposes, integrated recognition systems have been, and are still being developed. Chapter 5 provides an overview of such major recognition systems including their particular key features.

Finally, in Chap. 6 we will give a concluding discussion on the state-of-the-art of Markov-model based handwriting recognition. This comprises the latest technological trends, some remarks on benchmarking and reporting results, and a short discussion of future challenges we identified for the field of MM-based HWR.

References

1. Arica N, Yarman-Vural FT (2001) An overview of character recognition focused on off-line handwriting. IEEE Trans on Syst Man Cybern Part C Appl Rev 31(2):216–232
2. Bunke H (2003) Recognition of cursive Roman handwriting—Past, present and future. In: Proceedings of international conference on document analysis and recognition, Edinburgh, Scotland, vol 1, pp 448–459
3. Fujisawa H (2008) Forty years of research in character and document recognition—an industrial perspective. Pattern Recognit 41:2435–2446
4. Plamondon R, Srihari SN (2000) On-line and off-line handwriting recognition: a comprehensive survey. IEEE Trans on Pattern Anal and Mach Intell 22(1):63–84
5. Vinciarelli A (2002) A survey on off-line cursive word recognition. Pattern Recognit 35:1433–1446
6. Pittman JA (2007) Handwriting recognition: tablet PC text input. IEEE Comput 40(9):49–54
7. Lang KJ, Waibel AH, Hinton GE (1990) A time-delay neural network architecture for isolated word recognition. Neural Netw 3(1):23–43
8. Guyon I, Albrecht P, Le Cun Y, Denker J, Hubbard W (1991) Design of a neural network character recognizer for a touch terminal. Pattern Recognit 24:105–119
9. Davis R (2007) Magic paper: sketch-understanding research. IEEE Comput 40(9):34–41
10. El Abed H, Märgner V (2011) ICDAR 2009—Arabic handwriting recognition competition. Int J Document Anal Recognit 14:3–13
11. Mondal T, Bhattacharya U, Parui S, Das K, Mandalapu D (2010) On-line handwriting recognition of Indian scripts—The first benchmark. In: Proceedings of the international conference on frontiers in handwriting recognition, Kolkata, India, pp 200–205
12. Jaeger S, Liu CL, Nakagawa M (2003) The state of the art in Japanese online handwriting recognition compared to techniques in western handwriting recognition. Int J Document Anal Recognit 6:75–8

13. Liu CL, Jaeger S, Nakagawa M (2004) Online recognition of Chinese characters: the state-of-the-art. IEEE Trans Pattern Anal Mach Intell 26(2):198–213
14. Schambach MP, Rottland J, Alary T (2008) How to convert a Latin handwriting recognition system to Arabic. In: Proceedings of the international conference on frontiers in handwriting recognition, Montréal, Canada
15. Markov AA (1913) Example of statistical investigations of the text of „Eugen Onegin", wich demonstrates the connection of events in a chain. In: Bulletin de l'Académie Impériale des Sciences de St.-Pétersbourg, Sankt-Petersburg, Russia, pp 153–162 (in Russian)
16. Baum L, Petrie T (1966) Statistical inference for probabilistic functions of finite state Markov chains. Ann Math Statist 37:1554–1563
17. Baum L, Petrie T, Soules G, Weiss N (1970) A maximization technique occurring in the statistical analysis of probabilistic functions of Markov chains. Ann Math Statist 41:164–171
18. Viterbi A (1967) Error bounds for convolutional codes and an asymptotically optimum decoding algorithm. IEEE Trans Inf Theory 13:260–269
19. Young S (1996) A review of large-vocabulary continuous-speech recognition. IEEE Signal Process Mag 13(9):45–57
20. Kaltenmeier A, Caesar T, Gloger JM, Mandler E (1993) Sophisticated topology of hidden Markov models for cursive script recognition. In: Proceedings of the international conference on document analysis and recognition, Tsukuba Science City, Japan, pp 139–142
21. Schwartz R, LaPre C, Makhoul J, Raphael C, Zhao Y (1996) Language-independent OCR using a continuous speech recognition system. In: Proceedings of the international conference on pattern recognition, Vienna, Austria, vol 3, pp 99–103
22. Vinciarelli A, Bengio S, Bunke H (2004) Offline recognition of unconstrained handwritten texts using HMMs and statistical language models. IEEE Trans Pattern Anal Mach Intell 26(6):709–720
23. Britto AdS, Sabourin R, Bortolozzi F, Suen CY (2001) A two-stage HMM-based system for recognizing handwritten numeral strings. In: Proceedings of the international conference on document analysis and recognition, Seattle, USA, pp 396–400
24. Gauthier N, Artières T, Dorizzi B, Ballinari P (2001) Strategies for combining on-line and off-line information in an on-line handwriting recognition system. In: Proceedings of the international conference on document analysis and recognition, Seattle, USA, pp 412–416
25. Ge Y, Huo Q (2002) A study on the use of CDHMM for large vocabulary offline recognition of handwritten Chinese characters. In: Proceedings of the international workshop on frontiers in handwriting recognition, Niagara on the Lake, Canada, pp 334–338
26. Nopsuwanchai R, Biem A, Clocksin WF (2006) Maximization of mutual information for offline Thai handwriting recognition. IEEE Trans Pattern Anal Mach Intell 28(8):1347–1351
27. Liwicki M, Bunke H (2008) Recognition of whiteboard notes: online, offline and combination. Machine Perception and Artificial Intelligence. World Scientific Publishing Company, Singapore
28. Plötz T, Thurau C, Fink GA (2008) Camera-based whiteboard reading: New approaches to a challenging task. In: Proceedings of the international conference on frontiers in handwriting recognition, Montreal, Canada, pp 385–390
29. Vajda S, Plötz T, Fink GA (2009) Layout analysis for camera-based whiteboard notes. J Univers Comput Sci 15(18):3307–3324
30. Wienecke M, Fink GA, Sagerer G (2003) Towards automatic video-based whiteboard reading. In: Proceedings of the international conference on document analysis and recognition, IEEE, Edinburgh, Scotland, pp 87–91
31. Wienecke M, Fink GA, Sagerer G (2005) Toward automatic video-based whiteboard reading. Int J Document Anal Recognit 7(2–3):188–200
32. Fierrez J, Ortega-Garcia J, Ramos D, Gonzalez-Rodriguez J (2007) HMM-based on-line signature verification: feature extraction and signature modeling. Pattern Recognit Lett 28(16):2325–2334

33. Bao LV, Garcia-Salicetti S, Dorizzi B (2007) On using the Viterbi path along with HMM likelihood information for online signature verification. IEEE Trans Syst Man Cybern Part B Cybern 37(5):1237–1247

34. Brakensiek A, Rottland J, Rigoll G (2002) Handwritten address recognition with open vocabulary using character n-grams. In: Proceedings of the international workshop on frontiers in handwriting recognition, Niagara on the Lake, Canada, pp 357–362

35. Koerich AL, Leydier Y, Sabourin R, Suen CY (2002) A hybrid large vocabulary handwritten word recognition system using neuronal networks with hidden Markov models. In: Proceedings of the international workshop on frontiers in handwriting recognition, Niagara on the Lake, Canada, pp 99–104

36. Pechwitz M, Märgner V (2003) HMM based approach for handwritten Arabic word recognition using the IFN/ENIT-database. In: Proceedings of the international conference on document analysis and recognition, Edinburgh, Scotland, vol 2, pp 890–894

37. Vajda S, Belaid A (2005) Structural information implant in a context based segmentation-free HMM handwritten word recognition system for Latin and Bangla scripts. In: Proceedings of the international conference on document analysis and recognition, Seoul, Korea, vol 2, pp 1126–1130

38. Miletzki U, Bayer T, Schäfer H (1999) Continuous learning systems: postal address readers with built-in learning capability. In: Proceedings of the international conference on document analysis and recognition, Bangalore, India, pp 329–332

39. Schambach MP (2005) Fast script word recognition with very large vocabulary. In: Proceedings of the international conference on document analysis and recognition, Seoul, Korea, vol 1, pp 9–13

40. Morita M, El Yacoubi A, Sabourin R, Bortolozzi F, Suen CY (2001) Handwritten month word recognition on Brazilian bank cheques. In: Proceedings of the international conference on document analysis and recognition, Seattle, USA, pp 972–976

41. Xu Q, Kim JH, Lam L, Suen CY (2002) Recognition of handwritten month words on bank cheques. In: Proceedings of the international workshop on Frontiers in handwriting recognition, Niagara on the Lake, Canada, pp 111–116

42. Coetzer J, Herbst BM, du Preez JA (2004) Offline signature verification using the discrete Radon transform and a hidden Markov models. EURASIP J Appl Signal Process 4:559–571

43. Coetzer J, Herbst BM, du Preez JA (2006) Off-line signature verification: A comparison between human and machine performance. In: Proceedings of the international workshop on frontiers in handwriting recognition, La Baule, France, pp 481–486

44. Justino EJR, El Yacoubi A, Bortolozzi F, Sabourin R (2000) An off-line signature verification system using hidden Markov model and cross-validation. In: Proceedings of XIII Brazilian symposium on computer graphics and image processing, Gramado, Brazil, pp 105–112

45. Marti UV, Bunke H (2001b) Text line segmentation and word recognition in a system for general writer independent handwriting recognition. In: Proceedings of the international conference document analysis and recognition, Seattle, USA, pp 159–163

46. Zimmermann M, Bunke H (2002a) Automatic segmentation of the IAM off-line database for handwritten English text. In: Proceedings of the international conference on pattern recognition, Montréal, Canada, vol 4, pp 35–39

47. Chen M, Ding X, Wu Y (2003) Unified HMM-based layout analysis framework and algorithm. Sci China Ser F Inf Sci 46:401–408 10.1360/02yf0135

48. e Silva A (2009) Learning rich hidden Markov models in document analysis: table location. In: Proceedings of the international conference on document analysis and recognition, Barcelona, Spain, pp 843–847

49. Zou J, Le D, Thoma GR (2007) Online medical journal article layout analysis. In: Lin X, Yanikoglu BA (eds) Document recognition and retrieval XIV, SPIE

Chapter 2
General Architecture

Abstract As a first step of document understanding a digital image of the document to be analyzed or the trajectory of the pen used for writing needs to be captured. From this raw data the relevant document elements (e.g., text lines) need to be segmented. These are then subject to a number of pre-processing steps that aim at reducing the variability in the appearance of the writing by applying a sequence of normalization operations. In order to be processed by a handwriting recognition system based on Markov models, text-line images and raw pen trajectories are then converted into a sequential representation—which is quite straight-forward for online data but requires some "trick" in the offline case. Based on the serialized data representation features are computed that characterize the local appearance of the script. These are fed into a Markov-model based decoder that produces a hypothesis for the segmentation *and* classification of the analyzed portion of handwritten text—usually as a sequence of word or character hypotheses.

Keywords Handwriting recognition [overview] · System architecture · Segmentation free recognition · Serialization · Pre-processing · Feature extraction · Model decoding

Any handwriting recognition system is usually embedded into a larger document analysis framework, e.g., a mail-sorting machine or a pen-based computer interface. Necessarily, as a first step of document understanding a digital image of the document to be analyzed or the trajectory of the pen used for writing needs to be captured by some device, e.g., a scanner, a camera, or a digitizer tablet. In general, the data capturing process may record also undesired document content besides the desired text, which—in the online case—is usually avoided by the user interface. When handwritten documents are processed offline, however, the captured image usually shows also other document structures (e.g., tables, figures, or images) or even non-document parts of the scene background. Therefore, in general the relevant document

T. Plötz and G. A. Fink, *Markov Models for Handwriting Recognition*,   9
SpringerBriefs in Computer Science, DOI: 10.1007/978-1-4471-2188-6_2,
© Thomas Plötz 2011

Original Image   Alternative segmentations

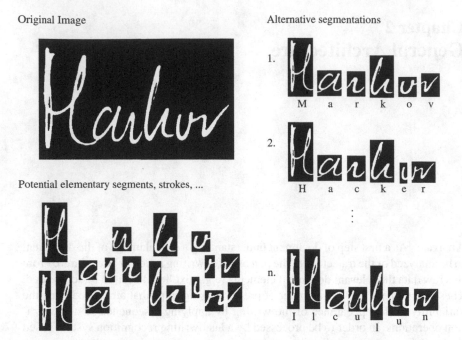

Potential elementary segments, strokes, ...

Fig. 2.1 Example of classical HWR approach relying on explicit segmentation and subsequent classification (inspired by [2])

elements (e.g., text lines or paragraphs) need to be segmented[1] from the captured input data. As soon as portions of handwritten text have been identified in the input, these can be further segmented into text-lines or even words. These are then subject to a number of pre-processing steps that aim at reducing the variability in the appearance of the writing by applying a sequence of normalization operations.

A classical HWR system would then proceed by attempting to segment the normalized text into candidates of primitives (e.g., strokes or characters, see Fig. 2.1). The potential primitives would then be classified and the best segmentation result would be selected—usually according to some heuristic. In contrast to this approach, MM-based HWR systems can avoid carrying out segmentation[2] at the level of character sequences and subsequent classification separately. The only requirement for

---

[1] Especially when processing machine printed documents where it is usually clear that the document image only shows the document to be analyzed, this initial segmentation of relevant document structures is referred to as layout analysis (cf., e.g., [1]).

[2] As any document analysis system needs to extract relevant textual items, e.g., words or lines, from the document image or the raw pen trajectory prior to recognition, several preprocessing steps are necessary. These perform tasks which can also be termed "segmentation". Though there are first approaches to perform, e.g., line separations using HMMs [3], in this respect traditional and MM-based systems are still quite similar. Therefore, in this book we focus on the segmentation at the level of character or word sequences where MM-based approaches can show their strengths.

their application is that the data to be processed must be representable as a sequence of items *without* making decisions about potential segmentations.

Therefore, after normalization text-line images and raw pen trajectories are converted into a sequential representation—which is quite straight-forward for online data but requires some "trick" in the offline case. Based on the serialized data representation local features are computed. The feature vector sequences obtained are then fed into an MM-based decoder that produces a hypothesis for the segmentation *and* classification of the analyzed portion of handwritten text—usually as a sequence of word or character hypotheses.

The complete pipeline of processing steps applied in a state-of-the-art HWR system based on Markov models is shown in Fig. 2.2. It largely follows a standard pattern recognition approach comprising preprocessing, feature extraction, and classification (cf., e.g., [5]). What is special for MM-based HWR systems is that a serialization of the patterns to be recognized is carried out prior to feature extraction and that segmentation and classification are achieved in an integrated manner by the joint decoding of HMMs and n-gram models.

2.1 Text-Line Extraction

In most applications of HWR it is ensured that the document capturing process delivers an image or a raw pen trajectory of the desired document only. In pen-based computer interfaces handwritten input is usually required to be entered within a special input field, making sure that a single character, word, or text line is captured. Within document images acquired offline, however, paragraphs of text need to be localized and lines of text need to be extracted. The methods applied usually rely on the assumption that handwritten text is oriented approximately horizontally and is organized in line structures. Individual lines of text can then be extracted by, for example, analyzing horizontal projection histograms or by applying probabilistic segmentation techniques (cf. [6]). A good overview of algorithms for text-line extraction from document images is given in [7].

2.2 Pre-Processing

Images or raw trajectories of handwritten text usually vary with respect to baseline orientation (frequently also referred to as skew), slant angle, and size of the handwriting. Therefore, almost all HWR systems apply pre-processing operations that attempt to normalize the appearance of the writing with respect to these three aspects (cf., e.g., [8, 9]). In addition, normalization operations are applied, which are special for the representation of handwriting data as either pen trajectories or text line images.

In contrast to online processing, where the capturing process more-or-less guarantees that the writing is clearly separated from the document background, in document

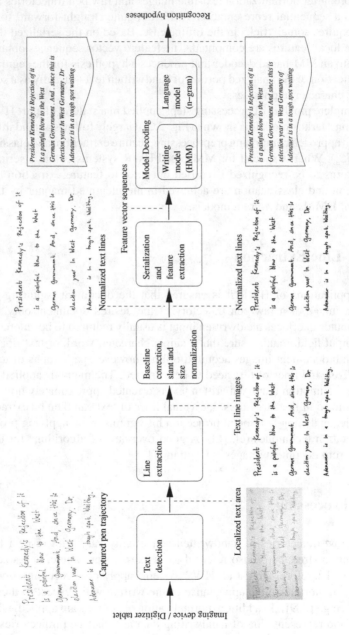

Fig. 2.2 Schematic overview of the typical architecture of an HMM-based handwriting recognition system. Example data (document images, raw and resampled pen trajectories) taken from IAM-OnDB^{Cam} and IAM-OnDB, respectively (cf. Sect. 5.1), used with permission. Line extraction, pre-processed data, and recognition hypotheses by the authors (cf. [4]).

images the ink trace has yet to be recovered from the raw image data. Therefore, the word or text line images are binarized—either before applying other pre-processing steps or during some phase of pre-processing—thus separating dark ink pixels from the document's background (cf., e.g., [10]).

Even though online handwriting data is captured by special devices there may be errors introduced by the recording process. Therefore, online data usually is subject to some heuristic smoothing operations in order to compensate potential jitter or other imperfections present in the raw trajectory data (cf., e.g., [11, 12]). In addition, capturing the writing process online also provides information about the speed of the writing, which—with the exception of signature verification—is not relevant for handwriting recognition. Consequently, raw pen trajectories are frequently subject to a resampling step where the original trajectory is replaced by a dense sequence of equidistantly spaced points (cf., e.g., [9]).

In order to compensate for an unknown baseline orientation or skew angle, either the baseline orientation itself or a suitable approximation thereof is usually computed and subsequently compensated by appropriately rotating the line image or the raw pen trajectory. The methods applied are somewhat script dependent. For example, computing a baseline estimate by interpolating local contour minima (cf. [13, 14])— which is equally applicable for both online and offline data—works well for Roman script, but will be likely to fail for Arabic. More widely applicable is the implicit estimation of the baseline orientation by maximizing the entropy of the horizontal projection histogram (cf., e.g., [15]).

The slant angle, i.e., the tilt of individual handwritten characters with respect to the vertical, is compensated by applying a shear transform to the text-line image or to the raw pen trajectory. The crucial part here is the reliable estimation of the slant angle. For online data this estimate can be determined from a histogram of orientations of all line segments connecting two adjacent trajectory points (cf., e.g., [9]). In offline processing many successful methods rely on gradient information extracted from the text-line image (cf., e.g., [16, 17]).

No generally accepted methodology exists so far for the normalization of the apparent size of handwriting. HWR systems that compute the baseline and other writing lines often rely on an estimate of the so-called core size, i.e., the size of lower-case letters in Roman script (cf., e.g., [9, 18, 19]). However, as size normalization is quite crucial, any error in estimating the writing lines will lead to an inappropriate size normalization and consequently to the almost inevitable failure of the subsequent recognition process. A quite robust method for normalizing the size of Roman script was proposed in [20] which uses an estimate of average character width. For online HWR a size independent representation of the pen-trajectory data was proposed in [21].

2.3 Serialization

MM-based recognizers require the data to be analyzed to be sequentially or temporally ordered. Therefore, a suitable technique for converting the pre-processed samples of handwriting into a sequential representation is an integral part of any MM-based HWR system.

Achieving such a serialization for the online case seems trivial at first as the recorded pen trajectory data consists of a temporally ordered set of pen positions. However, there are cases where the temporal order of the pen trajectory may deviate from the logical serial order of the characters written. In Roman script this is the case for the placement of diacritic marks as, e.g., the dots of the character "i" or the German umlauts ("ä", "ö", "ü"), or for the French accents (e.g., "é"). Here the actual diacritic mark may be written at almost any time after the base-character resulting in a so-called *delayed stroke* which may be separated from the associated base-character by other script elements. In order to preserve the correspondence between the temporal order of the pen trajectory and the logical order of characters in words the removal of such delayed strokes was first proposed in [14] and later became a widely used technique in online HWR systems (cf., e.g., [9, 21]). As information is lost by removing even small parts of the script this operation is never applied in isolation but only in conjunction with a suitable compensation within the feature representation computed (cf. Sect. 4.2).

In offline HWR serialization of the data is a major problem as two-dimensional images of words or text-lines need to be processed. The central idea behind the principal serialization method for offline handwriting data—the so-called *sliding-window* approach—is to convert the word or text-line images into a sequence of local image representations following the logical order of characters. This basic method was first proposed for offline handwriting recognition by researchers at Daimler-Benz Research Center [22]. Later, the method was pioneered by BBN especially for offline recognition of machine-printed text [23]. It consists of sliding a small analysis window, which usually is only a few pixels wide (i.e., much narrower than a character image), along the text-line image, i.e., in the direction of the writing. Thus small vertical stripes are extracted from the text-line image which usually overlap to some degree (see Fig. 2.3). This sequence of image stripes forms the basis of the subsequent feature extraction.

2.4 Feature Extraction

The general goal of feature extraction methods to be used in conjunction with HMM-based recognizers is to extract parametric representations of the local appearance of the script from the input handwriting data. In order to describe the local shape of pen trajectories—e.g., by computing local orientation and curvature—the pre-processed trajectories are split into small segments[3] according to some simple heuristic rule, e.g., by extracting fixed-length segments from resampled data or by splitting the

---

[3] The very basic splitting of the input data at this early stage is fundamentally different from the much more complex segmentation of handwriting data into meaningful parts as, e.g., characters or words. See also Sect. 4.1 for a discussion.

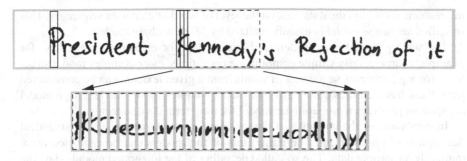

Fig. 2.3 Example of the sliding-window approach: above, the text line to be analyzed is shown with some of the overlapping analysis windows superimposed. Below, the extracted image stripes are shown for part of the text line. Note, the width of the analysis windows was set to 10 pixels in this illustratory example in order to increase legibility. Usually narrower stripes are used. Example based on a document image taken from IAM-OnDB^Cam (cf. Sect. 5.1), used with permission, pre-processed by the authors.

trajectory into stroke-like segments at points where the vertical writing speed is minimum (cf. [21]). Usually, these trajectory segments overlap to some degree in order not to introduce artifacts into the feature representation resulting from boundary effects.

For HMM-based offline HWR feature extraction methods directly build on the results of the sliding-window analysis of the word or text-line images. The computation of local shape representations is less straight-forward than in the online case as these local descriptions need to be extracted from small image stripes. Usually, either statistical image descriptors as, e.g., moments or histograms are computed or some heuristically defined method for extracting basic geometrical properties is applied.

Taken together, the methods for producing local views on the data—i.e., the basic splitting-up of pen trajectories into segments and the sliding-window technique for handwriting images—and the feature extraction methods applied to each trajectory segment or analysis window, respectively, compute a local description of the appearance of the script to be analyzed. Therefore, the procedure can principally be compared to the short-time analysis and feature computation as applied for the purpose of speech recognition, though —especially in the case of the sliding-window technique—it lacks a clear justification from a signal-theoretic point of view.

2.5 Modeling and Decoding

For reasons that will be detailed in the following section, recognition systems based on Markov models use two distinct modeling components. The appearance of the handwriting as defined by its local characteristics captured in the feature representation is described by hidden Markov models. We will refer to this modeling component as the *writing model*. The second modeling component describes long term sequencing restrictions within the data, i.e., on the level of word or character sequences. This so-called *language model* is usually realized by Markov chain models.

The writing model usually defines basic models for elementary units like, for example, characters. By simple combination operations, more complex model structures for, e.g., arbitrary sequences of words from a given lexicon, can be constructed from these basic entities quite easily. In such a complex model the language model component provides a probabilistic model for long term dependencies.

In combination, the writing and the language model form a powerful statistical description of handwriting. The parameters of the models can be estimated automatically on sample data. The so-called decoding of the integrated model—i.e., the search for the optimal path through the combined state space—provides the optimal segmentation *and* classification of the data in an integrated framework.

References

1. Mao S, Rosenfeld A, Kanungo T (2003) Document structure analysis algorithms: a literature survey. In: Proceedings of SPIE electronic imaging, pp 197–207
2. Gader PD, Keller J M, Krishnapuram R, Chiang JH, Mohamed MA (1997) Neuronal and fuzzy methods in handwriting recognition. IEEE Comput 2:79–86
3. Lu Z, Schwartz R, Raphael C (2000) Script-independent, HMM-based text line finding for OCR. In: Proceedings of international conference on pattern recognition, Barcelona, Spain, pp 551–554
4. Plötz T, Thurau C, Fink GA (2008) Camera-based whiteboard reading: new approaches to a challenging task. In: Proceedings of international conference on frontiers in handwriting recognition, Montreal, Canada, pp 385–390
5. Duda RO, Hart PE, Stork DG (2000) Pattern classification, 2nd edn. Wiley Interscience, New York
6. Li Y, Zheng Y, Doermann D, Jaeger S (2008) Script-independent text line segmentation in freestyle handwritten documents. IEEE Trans Pattern Anal Mach Intell 30(8):1313–1329
7. Likforman-Sulem L, Zahour A, Taconet B (2007) Text line segmentation of historical documents: a survey. Int J Doc Anal Recognit 9(2):123–138
8. Fujisawa H (2007) Robustness design of industrial strength recognition systems. In: Chaudhuri B (ed) Digital document processing: major diretions and recent advances. Springer, London, pp 185–212
9. Jaeger S, Manke S, Reichert J, Waibel A (2001) Online handwriting recognition: the NPen++ recognizer. Int J Doc Anal Recognit 3:169–180
10. Trier OD, Taxt T (1995) Evaluation of binarization methods for document images. IEEE Trans Pattern Anal Mach Intell 17(3):312–315
11. Guerfali W, Plamondon R (1993) Normalizing and restoring on-line handwriting. Pattern Recognit 26(3):419–431
12. Tappert C, Suen C, Wakahara T (1990) The state of the art in on-line handwriting recognition. IEEE Trans Pattern Anal Mach Intell 12(8):787–808
13. Bozinovic RM, Srihari SN (1989) Off-line cursive script word recognition. IEEE Trans Pattern Anal Mach Intell 11(1):69–83
14. Schenkel M, Guyon I, Henderson D (1994) On-line cursive script recognition using time delay neural networks and hidden Markov models. In: Proceedings of international conference on acoustics, speech, and signal processing, Adelaide, Australia, vol 2, pp 637–640

15. Vinciarelli A, Luettin J (2001) A new normalization technique for cursive handwritten words. Pattern Recognit Lett 22(9):1043–1050
16. Bertolami R, Uchida S, Zimmermann M, Bunke H (2007) Non-uniform slant correction for handwritten text line recognition. In: Proceedings of international conference on document analysis and recognition, Curitiba, Brazil, vol 1, pp 18–22
17. Ding Y, Kimura F, Miyake Y, Shridhar M (2000) Accuracy improvement of slant estimation for handwritten words. In: Proceedings of international conference on pattern recognition, Barcelona, Spain, vol 4, pp 527–530
18. Cai J, Liu ZQ (2000) Off-line unconstrained handwritten word recognition. Int J Pattern Recognit Artif Intell 14(3):259–280
19. Marti UV, Bunke H (2000) Handwritten sentence recognition. In: Proceedings of international conference on pattern recognition, Barcelona, Spain, vol 3, pp 467–470
20. Madhvanath S, Kim G, Govindaraju V (1999) Chaincode contour processing for handwritten word recognition. IEEE Trans Pattern Anal Mach Intell 21(9):928–932
21. Dolfing JGA, Haeb-Umbach R (1997) Signal representations for Hidden Markov Model based on-line handwriting recognition. In: Proceedings of international conference on acoustics, speech, and signal processing, Munich, Germany, vol 4, pp 3385–3388
22. Caesar T, Gloger JM, Mandler E (1993) Preprocessing and feature extraction for a handwriting recognition system. In: Proceedings of international conference on document analysis and recognition, Tsukuba Science City, Japan, pp 408–411
23. Schwartz R, LaPre C, Makhoul J, Raphael C, Zhao Y (1996) Language-independent OCR using a continuous speech recognition system. In: Proceedings of international conference on pattern recognition, Vienna, Austria, vol 3, pp 99–103

Chapter 3
Markov Model Concepts: The Essence

Abstract The integrated use of hidden Markov models (HMMs) and Markov chain models can be considered the state-of-the-art for the analysis of sequential data. The former represents a generative model that covers the "appearance" of the underlying data whereas the latter describes restrictions of possible hypotheses sequences. Hidden Markov models describe a two-stage stochastic process with hidden states and observable outputs. The first stage can be interpreted as a probabilistic finite state automaton, which is the basis for the generative modeling as it is described by the second stage. Markov chain models are usually realized as stochastic n-gram models, which describe the probability of the occurrence of entire symbol sequences. For both HMMs and Markov chain models efficient algorithms exist for parameter estimation and for model evaluation. They can be used in an integrated manner for effective segmentation and classification of sequential data. This chapter gives a detailed overview of the theoretical foundations of Markovian models as they are used for handwriting recognition.

Keywords Theory · Algorithms · Definition · Recognition paradigm · Segmentation free recognition · Mixture model · Hidden Markov model · n-gram model

For the analysis of sequential data, the use of hidden Markov models (HMMs) as statistical models can be considered the state-of-the-art. In combination with Markov-chain models, which describe restrictions of possible hypotheses sequences, powerful classification systems can be realized. For online recognition handwriting data is of sequential type by its nature since it is recorded as the text is written and, thus, corresponds to time series. Images of handwriting, as processed by offline recognizers, can be transferred into a sequential representation by moving a sliding window along the particular text lines (cf. Sect. 2.3). Thus, Markov models are a perfect fit for handwriting recognition.

The following summary of the theoretical concepts behind Markov models is mainly adopted from the argumentation in [1]. An abridged, tutorial-style version thereof with focus on handwriting recognition can be found in [2]. The inter-

T. Plötz and G. A. Fink, *Markov Models for Handwriting Recognition*,
SpringerBriefs in Computer Science, DOI: 10.1007/978-1-4471-2188-6_3,
© Thomas Plötz 2011

ested reader will find an in-depth treatment of MM-based pattern recognition
methods in [3].

3.1 Recognition Paradigm

Markov-model based recognition approaches are, generally, based on the assumption
of a statistical model for the generation of the data to be analyzed. A sequence
of symbols **w**—characters or words—generated by some source, i.e., the writing
process, is coded into a signal representation (for offline HWR this means images of
handwritten text) and later observed as a sequence of feature vectors **X**. Formally,
the goal of the recognition process is then to find the sequence $\hat{\mathbf{w}}$ that maximizes the
posterior probability $P(\mathbf{w}|\mathbf{X})$ of the symbol sequence given the data.

$$
\begin{aligned}
\hat{\mathbf{w}} &= \arg\max_{\mathbf{w}} P(\mathbf{w}|\mathbf{X}) = \arg\max_{\mathbf{w}} \frac{P(\mathbf{w})P(\mathbf{X}|\mathbf{w})}{P(\mathbf{X})} \\
&= \arg\max_{\mathbf{w}} P(\mathbf{w})P(\mathbf{x}|\mathbf{w})
\end{aligned}
\tag{3.1}
$$

When applying Bayes' rule $P(\mathbf{w}|\mathbf{X})$ can be rewritten into a form, where
the two modeling components of typical Markov-model based recognition systems
become manifest. $P(\mathbf{w})$ denotes the language model probability for the sequence
of symbols **w**. Technically, stochastic n-gram models represent the usual realization
of language models. $P(\mathbf{X}|\mathbf{w})$ represents the probability of observing the sequence
of symbols as features **X** according to the writing model, namely the HMM.

The fundamental advantage of Markov-model based recognizers is that they do not
require an explicit segmentation of the data prior to its classification. The recognition
is thus performed in a *segmentation-free* manner, which means that segmentation
and classification are integrated. Thus, the application of Markov models to pre-
segmented input data, as described in some publications, appears to make sense only
for very rare special cases, if any.

3.2 Hidden Markov Models

3.2.1 Definition

HMMs describe a two-stage stochastic process with hidden states and observable
outputs. The first stage represents a discrete stochastic process, which produces a
series of random variables that take on values from a discrete set of states. This
process is *stationary*, which means that its statistical properties do not change over
time, and it is also *causal* and *simple*. The last two properties taken together restrict
the dependency of the probability distributions of states generated by the random

variables to be dependent on the immediate predecessor state only. The Markov process is then said to be of first order.

$$P(s_t|s_1, s_2, \ldots, s_{t-1}) = P(s_t|s_{t-1}) \tag{3.2}$$

Basically, this first stage represents a finite state automaton, which behaves probabilistically. In the second stage then at every time t an output O_t is generated depending on the current state s_t only:

$$P(O_t|O_1 \ldots O_{t-1}, s_1 \ldots s_t) = P(O_t|s_t) \tag{3.3}$$

Since only these outputs O_t, and not the associated internal states s_t, can be observed, the overall model is referred to as *hidden* Markov model.

In summary, a *first order* HMM λ is formally defined as consisting of:

- a finite set of states $\{s|1 \le s \le N\}$,
- a matrix of state transition probabilities[1] $\mathbf{A} = \{a_{ij}|a_{ij} = P(s_t = j|s_{t-1} = i)\}$,
- a vector of start probabilities $\pi = \{\pi_i|\pi_i = P(s_1 = i)\}$, and
- state-specific output probability distributions $\{b_j(O_t)|b_j(O_t) = p(O_t|s_t = j)\}$ for discrete outputs or $\{b_j(\mathbf{x})|b_j(\mathbf{x}) = p(\mathbf{x}|s_t = j)\}$ for continuous modeling, respectively (see below).

3.3 Modeling Outputs

Depending on the type of input data, the output elements generated per state can be either symbolic—i.e., of discrete type—or continuous. The latter representation is better suited for handwriting recognition purposes, as usually real-valued vectors $\mathbf{x}$ from some high-dimensional feature-space $\mathbb{R}^N$, which is derived from the original handwriting data, are processed. Consequently, the probability distributions $p(\mathbf{x}|s_t = j)$ of the statistical outputs of the model need to be able to define continuous distributions over $\mathbb{R}^N$. Since no general parametric families of such distributions are known, in the continuous case probability distributions are usually approximated via state-specific mixtures of Gaussians:

$$p(\mathbf{x}|s_t = j) \doteq \sum_{k=1}^{\infty} c_{jk} \mathcal{N}(\mathbf{x}|\boldsymbol{\mu}_{jk}, \mathbf{C}_{jk}) \approx \sum_{k=1}^{M} c_{jk} \mathcal{N}(\mathbf{x}|\boldsymbol{\mu}_{jk}, \mathbf{C}_{jk}) \tag{3.4}$$

where $\mathcal{N}(\mathbf{x}|\boldsymbol{\mu}_{jk}, \mathbf{C}_{jk})$ denotes a Gaussian normal distribution with mean vector $\boldsymbol{\mu}_{jk}$ and covariance matrix $\mathbf{C}_{jk}$, and c_{jk} represents the prior probability of the kth mixture.

---

[1] For practical applications the actual model topology—i.e., the connectivity between states of a certain model—is usually limited using specific, non-ergodic model architectures (e.g., linear or Bakis type).

As for continuous HMMs the number of parameters is drastically increased with respect to the discrete case. Several techniques were developed to reduce the number of parameters by jointly using parts of the model. Such methods are usually referred to as *tying* of parameters. The most well-known of these approaches are the so-called *semi-continuous HMMs*—also frequently referred to as *tied-mixture models* [4, 5]. In such models only a single set of component densities is used to construct all state-specific output probability densities:

$$b_j(\mathbf{x}) = \sum_{k=1}^{M} c_{jk} \mathcal{N}(\mathbf{x}|\boldsymbol{\mu}_k, \mathbf{C}_k) \tag{3.5}$$

3.3.1 Algorithms

The attractiveness of HMMs is to a large extent justified by the fact that efficient algorithms for estimating the model parameters as well as for decoding the model on new data exist. Decoding corresponds to the integrated segmentation and classification of the associated data.

A variant of the well-known Expectation Maximization (EM) technique [6], namely the so-called Baum-Welch algorithm is commonly used for training the model. The method applies an iterative growth transformation to the model parameters such that the generation probability of the data given the model is improved:

$$P(\mathbf{O}|\hat{\lambda}) \geq P(\mathbf{O}|\lambda) \tag{3.6}$$

Here $\hat{\lambda}$ denotes the adapted HMM derived from the previous model λ by applying one re-estimation step to the parameters. Model training is iterated until convergence is reached, i.e., until $P(\mathbf{O}|\hat{\lambda}) - P(\mathbf{O}|\lambda) \leq \varepsilon$ for some small threshold ε.

Traditionally HMM-based modeling follows a generative approach by deriving model parameters that maximize the likelihood of the training data. Consequently, the goal of the parameter estimation procedure is to derive a representation, which describes the probability distributions of the pattern classes it is modeling in the best possible way. In contrast to approximating the shapes of pattern classes, discriminative modeling techniques aim at maximum separation between different classes. Therefore, some less strict criteria are optimized like, e.g., maximum mutual information or minimum error rate (cf. [7, 8]), or combinations of both [9]. In the field of HMM-based (online) handwriting recognition, e.g., [10] describes a training procedure based on the optimization of the minimum classification error.

The basis of model decoding is formed by the so-called Viterbi algorithm, which is used to—in the statistical sense—"infer" the hidden state sequence $\mathbf{s}^*$ that with maximum probability generates an available sequence of outputs given the model:

$$\mathbf{s}^* = \arg\max_{\mathbf{s}} P(\mathbf{O}, \mathbf{s}|\lambda) \tag{3.7}$$

As states can be associated with basic segmentation units—for HWR usually this corresponds to characters—decoding yields the segmentation of the data considered on the basis of the current model.

3.3.2 Practical Issues

The efficiency in both evaluating and decoding the model arises from the fact that HMMs store only one internal state as context for future actions, which is also called the Markov property. Therefore, computations necessary to obtain the production probability $P(\mathbf{O}|\lambda)$ and the optimal state sequence $\mathbf{s}^*$ can be performed in a dynamic programming style with linear complexity in the length of the sequence considered and quadratic complexity in the number of model states. Still, the algorithms are usually not efficient enough in practice. Hence, especially for decoding model pruning strategies like the beam-search algorithm [11] are applied.

In almost all current implementations of HMM-based recognizers (negative) logarithmic representations of probabilities are used. Thus, products of probabilities are turned into sums. Due to the reduced dynamic range of these additive costs, computations involving very small probabilities become numerically feasible even if such quantities are accumulated within large model architectures or for extremely long observation sequences.

3.4 N-gram Models

In addition to the analysis of local context within sequential data, which is covered by HMMs, it is desirable in many applications to be able to describe long-term dependencies within the statistical modeling framework. For HWR applications restrictions concerning the potential co-occurrences of subsequent characters or words (depending on the modeling basis) can not be captured reasonably using HMMs alone. This is where Markov-chain models come into play.

3.4.1 Definition

Markov-chain models can be used to statistically describe the probability of the occurrence of entire symbol sequences. Formally speaking [cf. (3.1)] the probability $P(\mathbf{w})$ of a sequence of symbols $\mathbf{w} = w_1, w_2, \ldots, w_T$ is calculated. In order to make things mathematically tractable, $P(\mathbf{w})$ is first factorized using Bayes' rule according to

$$P(\mathbf{w}) = P(w_1)P(w_2|w_1)\ldots P(w_T|w_1, \ldots, w_{T-1})$$

$$= \prod_{t=1}^{T} P(w_t|w_1, \ldots, w_{t-1}) \tag{3.8}$$

Since the context dependency increases arbitrarily with the length of the symbol sequence, in practice the "history" of a certain symbol is limited:

$$P(\mathbf{w}) \approx \prod_{t=1}^{T} P(\underbrace{w_t | w_{t-n+1}, \ldots, w_{t-1}}_{n \text{ symbols}}) \tag{3.9}$$

This means that the probability of the complete sequence is defined on the basis of the conditional probabilities of some symbol—or word—w_t occurring in the context of its $n - 1$ predecessor words $w_{t-n+1}, \ldots, w_{t-1}$. Markov-chain models are therefore often referred to as n-gram models.

3.4.2 Algorithms

For the evaluation of n-gram models on unknown data usually the perplexity $\mathscr{P}$

$$\mathscr{P}(\mathbf{w}) = \frac{1}{\sqrt[|\mathbf{w}|]{P(\mathbf{w})}} = \frac{1}{\sqrt[T]{P(w_1, w_2, \ldots, w_T)}}$$
$$= P(w_1, w_2, \ldots, w_T)^{-\frac{1}{T}} \tag{3.10}$$

is exploited as the evaluation criterion. Formally, the perplexity of some unseen data $\mathbf{w}$ follows the cross-entropy between the symbol distribution defined by the probabilistic model and the one defined empirically by the data. The smaller the perplexity, the better the n-gram model is able to predict the unseen data.

Parameter estimation for stochastic language models, i.e., training of n-gram models, is based on the determination of n-gram occurrences c in sample data. Conditional probabilities are calculated as the ratios of n-gram—or event—counts $c(w_1, w_2, \ldots, w_n)$ and those obtained for the respective contexts $c(w_1, w_2, \ldots, w_{n-1})$.

$$P(w_n | w_1, w_2, \ldots, w_{n-1}) = \frac{c(w_1, w_2, \ldots, w_n)}{c(w_1, w_2, \ldots, w_{n-1})} \tag{3.11}$$

3.4.3 Practical Issues

Even for moderate sizes of n (e.g., 2 for bi-gram models or 3 for tri-gram models), most n-gram events necessary for deriving robust statistical estimates will not be observed in a typical set of training data due to its limited size. If performing naive training as described in the previous section, conditional probabilities for events not observed in the training data (so-called unseen events) will erroneously be determined as being zero. However, zero-probabilities are only valid in very rare cases. Certain events being unseen generally need to be attributed to the fact that too few samples are available for parameter estimation. Therefore, for robust estimation of *n*-gram models, it is of fundamental importance to appropriately smooth the raw probability estimates. Note that typically not some, but most *n*-gram counts will be zero.

Thus, in practical applications *n*-gram counts are modified and some "probability mass" for unseen events is gathered, e.g., by certain discounting techniques. The resulting zero-probability is then redistributed to unseen events according to a more general distribution. Widely used examples of smoothing techniques are Backing-Off and Interpolation (cf., e.g., [12]).

3.5 Combination of Writing and Language Model

As HMMs and *n*-gram models are quite similar to each other, they can be combined rather easily into an integrated model (cf. (3.1)). However, as HMM and *n*-gram models usually describe the data on widely different levels of granularity—i.e., in units of words for the language model and in sub-character units for the writing model—the different scores need to be combined in a weighted manner:

$$P(\mathbf{w})^\rho P(\mathbf{X}|\mathbf{w}) \tag{3.12}$$

The optimum weight ρ for a certain model configuration needs to be determined experimentally in practice. Sometimes an additional bias term is also used to control the number of word or character hypotheses generated.

Furthermore, as *n*-gram models span considerably longer contexts than HMMs, the search procedures used for integrated model decoding also become more complex (cf., e.g., [3, Chap. 12]). Unfortunately, there is no formal way to predict the performance improvement to be expected from the use of a language model. However, when comparing recognition results achieved by applying language models with different perplexities on the test data, the word error rates—according to a "rule-of-thumb"—will be roughly proportional to the square root of the perplexities. A substantial violation of that relation always indicates a problem with the integration of the language model evaluation into the overall decoding procedure.

References

1. Fink GA, Plötz T (2008) Developing pattern recognition systems based on Markov models: the ESMERALDA framework. Pattern Recognit Image Anal 18(2):207–215
2. Fink GA, Plötz T (2007) Tutorial on Markov models for handwriting recognition. In: Proceedings of the international conference on document analysis and recognition, Curitiba
3. Fink GA (2008) Markov models for pattern recognition–from theory to applications. Springer, Heidelberg
4. Huang XD, Jack MA (1989) Semi-continuous hidden Markov models for speech signals. Comput Speech Lang 3(3):239–251

5. Huang XD, Ariki Y, Jack MA (1990) Hidden Markov models for speech recognition. Edinburgh University Press, Edinburgh
6. Dempster AP, Laird NM, Rubin DB (1977) Maximum likelihood from incomplete data via the EM algorithm. J Royal Stat Soc Ser B 39(1):1–22
7. Bishop CM (2006) Pattern recognition and machine learning. Springer, New York
8. Jebara T (2004) Machine learning: discriminative and generative. Kluwer Academic, Dordrecht
9. Lee JS, Park CH (2005) Discriminative training of hidden Markov models by multiobjective optimization for visual speech recognition. In: Proceedings of the IEEE international joint conference neural networks, Montréal
10. Biem A (2006) Minimum classification error training for online handwriting recognition. IEEE Trans Pattern Analy Mach Intell 28(7):1041–1051
11. Lowerre BT (1976) The HARPY speech recognition system. Ph.D. thesis, Department of Computer Science, Carnegie-Mellon University, Pittsburg, USA
12. Chen SF, Goodman J (1999) An empirical study of smoothing techniques for language modeling. Comput Speech Lang 13:359–394

Chapter 4
Markov Model Based Handwriting Recognition

Abstract Markov models are very popular for sequential data analysis tasks due to their clear and reliable statistical foundations combined with the existence of efficient and robust algorithms for both model training and evaluation. However, in order to build effective handwriting recognition systems based on Markovian models, it is mandatory to tailor the general Markovian recognition framework towards the particular application domain. In this chapter we describe the practical aspects of Markov model based handwriting recognition. This includes a detailed treatment of the segmentation issue, which is especially important for offline HWR. Furthermore, common concepts for feature extraction on handwriting data are discussed followed by the reflection of modeling aspects. The integration of language models into handwriting recognizers has become very popular. This chapter also discusses practical aspects for n-gram estimation and integration.

Keywords Segmentation-free versus segmentation-based · Feature extraction · Output modeling · Model architecture · Context-dependent models · Model adaptation · Integrated decoding

The attractiveness of Markov models for various pattern recognition applications is mainly reasoned by the clear and reliable statistical framework they are based on. Efficient algorithms for parameter estimation and model evaluation exist, which is an important pre-requisite for their practical use in real-world applications.

The popularity of Markov models also for handwriting recognition is based on these very arguments. However, recognizers which can be applied *successfully* to real handwriting recognition tasks require substantially more know-how than the basic concepts as described in the previous section. In the following we will discuss respective practical issues including reviews of the particular state-of-the-art as described in the literature.[1]

---

[1] Unfortunately, in the literature the important technical aspects of the modeling and algorithms used are quite frequently not given in sufficient detail. Therefore, we concentrate on those publications that make this information explicit.

T. Plötz and G. A. Fink, *Markov Models for Handwriting Recognition*,
SpringerBriefs in Computer Science, DOI: 10.1007/978-1-4471-2188-6_4,
© Thomas Plötz 2011

4.1 Segmentation-Free Versus Segmentation-Based Recognition

The process of automatic handwriting recognition can be considered as a classical pattern classification task. Sensory data is automatically assigned to those pattern classes to which it most likely belongs. Thereby the evaluation of stochastic models is performed on the level of distinguished basic modeling units from some limited inventory (words, characters, or graphemes). Because of its creation process, handwritten script corresponds to time-series data. Characters are written one after another, thereby exhibiting mutual dependencies and touching each other. Consequently, handwriting recognition especially needs to address segmentation issues.

The importance of the segmentation aspect is—independent of actually focusing on Markov-model based handwriting recognition or on some other recognition approach—considered in the vast majority of related document analysis literature. In this context it does not make any difference whether online or offline techniques are considered as both need to address segmentation in some way. Unfortunately, so far no consistent terminology has been established that is commonly used by the community. Since segmentation can be considered at various levels of handwriting analysis certain clarification is necessary to avoid misunderstandings. As an example it needs to be clarified whether segmentation is considered at the document-, line-, word-, or character-level—which does not always become clear in the particular argumentation.

In this respect Arica and Yaman-Vural in [1] discuss a proposal for a taxonomy very thoroughly. Comparable arguments can, for example, also be found in [2–4], just to mention some examples. They discriminate between external and internal segmentation for offline recognition applications. The former is considered as being the most critical part of document analysis in general. By subdividing a document into text and non-text regions external segmentation is a necessary step prior to the offline HWR process. Markov models have meanwhile also been applied successfully for even more general document analysis tasks w.r.t. layout segmentation (cf., e.g., [5]). However, external segmentation is not directly related to the actual handwriting recognition process and will thus not be covered by this book. As the basis for HWR systems we assume words or text lines (not characters) that have successfully been isolated by means of some appropriate layout analysis technique. The latter also includes online recognition procedures where lines, words, and characters are relatively easy to extract by applying stroke-related heuristics (cf., e.g., [6] for a brief survey on segmentation for online Arabic HWR).

The direct application of the classical pattern classification approach to isolated words, i.e., word-based recognition of handwritten script, leads to so-called holistic approaches (cf., e.g., [2] and the references therein for an introduction, and [7] for a survey on holistic approaches to both online and offline HWR). For the case of offline recognition the captured image of some word to be recognized is considered as an "entity in its whole" [2] and based on some lexicon the actual recognition is performed. In principle, the same approach can be used for online recognition as well. In this case, a pre-segmentation procedure would extract the contiguous pen trajectory that corresponds to words (including intra-word pen-up phases) and all further segmentation is similar to the offline approach. Despite its attractiveness due to its simplicity this procedure has one serious drawback. In most realistic applications not enough sample data will be available for robust modeling, which usually prevents its application to real-world recognition tasks.

The alternative to the aforementioned holistic word-based recognition approaches is the analysis of handwritten script at the level of individual characters, i.e., character-based modeling. Based on a limited set of building blocks—character models—word-models are created by concatenation of these basic units.[2] Character-based modeling corresponds to the standard approach for state-of-the-art MM-based handwriting recognition. There are, however, two variants of the basic procedure.

In the first case an explicit segmentation of the word image into smaller units, usually the characters it consists of, is performed. In the literature respective approaches are referred to as segmentation-based or as relying on some explicit segmentation. It is commonly agreed that it is extremely difficult, if not impossible, to correctly segment a word into its characters without knowing the word itself. Consequently, the basic dilemma of such procedures (cf., e.g., [8–12]) is that the subsequent classification step will be doomed if this explicit segmentation step fails. This problem is especially critical when processing noisy input data—as handwriting often is. Certain approaches have been proposed to alleviate the strict dependency of segmentation-based HWR on *correctly* subdividing words into the characters they consist of. As one example explicit over-segmentation is performed (cf., e.g., [13]) and based on some alignment technique (as, e.g., dynamic programming), the optimal "segmentation path" through the word to be recognized is extracted [14–17]. Alternatively multiple segmentation solutions are generated by variants of the segmentation technique and the "best" solution w.r.t. the overall recognition results is chosen [18].

By means of the aforementioned segmentation-based procedures Markov models have been applied rather successfully to handwriting recognition tasks. Various strategies were developed that allows one to cope with the critical dependency of such recognition systems on reasonable segmentation results. However, if processing pre-segmented data one of the fundamental strengths of Markov models is ignored. As known from different application fields of MM-based recognizers, most notably automatic speech recognition, the basic advantage of Markov models is to perform pattern classification in a segmentation-free manner. Respective procedures are also referred to as implicit segmentation approaches.

For segmentation-free recognition all base models, i.e., HMMs modeling the respective characters, are integrated into one large recognition model. Technically, this corresponds to a parallel connection of base models by integrating their respective states into a global state-space (see Fig. 4.1) and adding connections between the HMMs. Viterbi decoding of this global state-space for handwriting data results in the most probable path through all base models. Transitions between modeling units

---

[2] Note that the recognition of isolated characters corresponds to some very special application, which does not lie in the focus of this book.

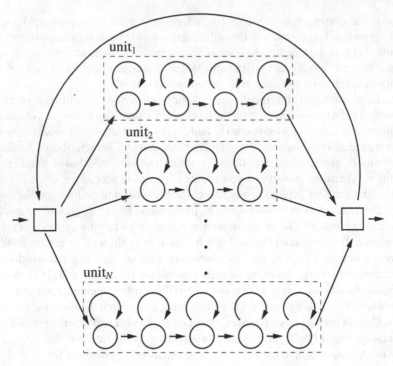

Fig. 4.1 Parallel connection of HMMs corresponding to certain basic modeling units, e.g., characters or words, for implicit segmentation during Viterbi-decoding. Transition between modeling units represent segment boundaries

along the path through the global state space correspond to the desired segmentation which is, thus, performed implicitly while classifying.

4.2 Feature Extraction

In virtually all applications, HWR using Markov models is based on certain feature representation of the input data. The motivation for this is twofold. First, some data-reduction is required since the number of parameters to be estimated during training is far too large for robust modeling if the grey-levels of image pixels or the coordinates of pen-trajectories are used directly. Second, despite the application of sophisticated pre-processing techniques that aim at producing a normalized version of the handwriting data to be analyzed, pre-processed script usually still exhibits substantial variance, which is mainly due to the considerable variations in writing style. Therefore, reasonable feature representations are mandatory that try to represent only the relevant information needed for discriminating between different units of the script to be analyzed.

Feature extraction methods for both online and offline HWR are based on a prior serialization of the data (cf. Sect. 2.3) and generally aim at computing a local representation of the appearance of the handwriting. Though there has been substantial research in both areas, for neither a standard feature set has been agreed upon, yet.

For online HWR features are computed that represent local characteristics of the pen trajectory in parametric form, most notably its slope and curvature (see, for example, [19, 20] for a description of a state-of-the-art feature set). These quantities are usually not directly represented as angles or changes thereof but are encoded by their sines and cosines in order to avoid discontinuities. In addition to local slope and curvature frequently the so-called *vicinity aspect* of the trajectory is computed. It corresponds to the height-to-width ratio of a bounding box containing a fixed number of trajectory points centered at the current position, i.e., the position's vicinity. In [20] features have been proposed that describe the trajectory's deviation from a straight line in that same vicinity. The so-called *curliness* is computed as the ratio of the total trajectory length within the vicinity to its maximum extension in either horizontal or vertical direction. The so-called *linearity* is defined as the average squared distance between trajectory points and a straight line connecting the first and last point in the vicinity. The latter can also be used to compute a more global estimate of the local writing direction.

Though absolute positions of trajectory points are not meaningful in general, frequently features based on pen positions after normalization are used, e.g., the normalized x and y coordinates. If baselines are estimated, also the relative vertical position with respect to the baseline can be used as a local feature. As during the online capturing of pen positions it is also known whether the pen is actually touching the writing surface or not, a feature encoding these pen-up phases is part of virtually every feature set for online HWR. More detailed measurements about the actual pen pressure or the local inclination of the pen with respect to the writing surface are, in contrast, only rarely used as they require rather special digitizer hardware.

A quite interesting technique for local shape representation in online HWR that to some extent bridges the gap to offline methods is given by the so-called *context bitmaps* [21]. They correspond to low-resolution images—only 3×3 pixels in size—of the handwriting centered at the current trajectory position. These small grey-level images are computed by rendering an offline image of the handwriting based on the trajectory data and extracting a down-sampled subimage with height and width equal to the estimate of the corpus height [20]. The features associated with the context bitmap directly correspond to the pixels' grey-levels of those images.

The feature representations computed for online HWR also play an important role in the handling of so-called *delayed strokes*. As described in Sect. 2.3 such strokes used for writing, e.g., accents of accented characters are usually removed during the serialization performed for online handwriting data [22]. The information lost is compensated on the level of the feature representation by introducing a so-called *hat feature* at the horizontal position in the pen trajectory corresponding to the position of the original delayed stroke (cf., e.g., [20, 23]).

Features for Markov-model based offline HWR are meant to encode the appearance of the script on the basis of the local views defined by the analysis windows extracted through the sliding-window framework (cf. Sect. 2.3). The methods applied can broadly be classified into being either statistical or structural. *Statistical features* are computed directly on the raw pixel intensities or on intensity distributions. *Structural features* are usually based on the analysis of certain geometrical properties. Combinations of these types of features aim at maximally benefiting from both kinds of information. Feature extraction methods not fitting into this classification scheme can hardly be found anymore.

According to the literature, the computation of certain statistical features directly on the particular pixel intensities, appears to be rather attractive for Markov model based HWR. Often pixel intensities or pixel density distributions—optionally their average or median values—are considered as some sort of basic features (as, e.g., in [9, 24–27]). For the so-called "percentile features" proposed in [28, 29] simply the cumulative histogram of the vertical distribution of ink pixels within an analysis window is computed. Quite frequently, starting from a certain raw feature set optimized representations are derived by some standard analytic transforms like PCA [15, 24, 27, 30–32], LDA [15, 33], or function transforms (DCT, FFT, Wavelet, Radon etc.) [25, 33, 34]. Based on raw pixel intensities, appearance based features like Eigen-projections can be derived as well [35].

In addition to statistical approaches various features have been proposed that are based on certain heuristic considerations. Many of them describe structural properties of handwriting like loops, ascenders, descenders [14], slopes [36], directional information [37], or concavity features [38]. In [39] a combination of several geometrical properties of the analysis windows are used as features.

In both online and offline HWR, and independently of the basic principle used for feature extraction, feature sets are frequently complemented by adding discrete approximations of the time-derivative of the individual vector components (cf., e.g., [23, 39, 40]). This technique, which is also widely used in automatic speech recognition, improves the ability of the final statistical sequence model to capture dynamic aspects of the data representation.

The process of feature extraction is critical for automatic handwriting recognition. This is especially the case for Markov-model based approaches. If the feature representation of handwritten data misses important properties, the recognition itself is likely to fail. In contrast, if too much redundancy is included by some feature representation, robust modeling becomes complicated when only limited sample sets are available for classifier training —as it is usually the case. In online HWR feature sets roughly consist of components representing the local trajectory characteristics as described above. However, up to date no standard feature set for online recognition has been agreed upon. In offline HWR, according to the literature, statistical and structural features are currently used in virtually equal shares. Since successful recognition systems have been developed based on both types of features it appears to be some sort of matter of taste which features to use. Therefore, in comparison to online HWR, in the field of offline recognition it is even less clear whether there might exist something like a universally accepted feature representation.

4.3 Building the Writing Model

In MM-based recognition systems the appearance of handwriting is analyzed using HMMs serving as writing models. Thereby, the regular case is the use of character models, which are concatenated to word models. For example, recognizers for Roman script contain models for upper and lower case letters, numerals, and those for punctuation symbols, which results in 70+ base models in total (cf., e.g., [33, 39, 40]). For Arabic recognizers substantially more models have to be used since Arabic uses 28 basic character shapes, which can appear realized quite differently in four types of contexts (cf. [41]).

The use of character models can limit the recognition performance of an HWR system. Therefore, some recognizers are based on an alternative modeling approach using graphemes as basic modeling units. Graphemes represent more fundamental units in handwriting ranging from single strokes to actual characters [42, p. 3f]. They are used for both Roman and Arabic script recognizers (cf., e.g., [15, 37, 43, 44]).

In some approaches different variants of graphemes—so-called allographs— are combined in multipath letter models with parallel state paths (cf., e.g., [45]). The advantage of this type of modeling units lies in the increased robustness of the resulting HMMs regarding writing style variations. As Arabic characters have different representations depending on their particular contexts (isolated, initial, medial, and final) a similar type of modeling can be used for Arabic recognizers [46].

4.3.1 Modeling Output Behavior

A fundamental question to be answered for HMM-based models is how the data is represented with respect to the statistical outputs generated by the HMM. The simplest way of specifying output distributions is by defining discrete probability distributions over some finite set of symbols. It is, however, quite cumbersome to define a coding of the inherently numeric feature representations of handwriting data into a symbol set. Therefore, today only very few approaches still make use of discrete HMMs operating on either discretely modeled distributions in feature space [13] or a hand-crafted symbolic coding of the data [9]. Very rarely discrete symbols are combined with continuous attributes for output modeling [47].

As the HMM-internal modeling is greatly simplified for discrete models, quite a number of approaches have been proposed that combine discrete HMMs with a vector quantization (VQ) step in order to be able to handle continuous feature representations (cf. [14, 25]). However, most methods of this type that are still in use today try to compensate the inherent limitations that arise from splitting up the model into two separate components. In [36] a fuzzy VQ is used to reduce the negative effects of quantization errors.

Other approaches combine HMMs and neuronal networks (NN) resulting in hybrid models. In [48] and related publications a NN-based VQ is combined with a discrete HMM with the advantage that it can be optimized jointly with the HMM parameters. In [43] the NN is used to directly compute the output probabilities of a continuous HMM. A similar hybrid system proposed in [49] was recently applied to large-vocabulary offline handwritten text recognition.

The majority of current handwriting recognition systems is based on continuous HMMs that describe output probability density distributions by mixtures of Gaussians [26, 27, 38, 50–53]. An important parameter of continuous density HMMs is the number of Gaussians used per state. As the sets of Gaussians are state specific and are not shared across the overall model this number is usually quite small. With the exception of [53] where 64 diagonal covariance Gaussians are used the number of Gaussians per state ranges between 3 and 12.

In order to construct more compact HWR systems and to use limited training data more effectively, instead of continuous HMMs with state-specific mixtures, tied-mixture HMMs are also frequently used [32, 39, 54–56]. In these systems the shared codebooks contain between several hundred component densities (e.g., 300 full-covariance Gaussians in [55]) and some thousand distributions (e.g., 1.5k diagonal-covariance Gaussians in [56]). Several more specific variants of mixture-tying with large numbers of overall densities used (up to approximately 150k) are explored in [40].

Even more parameter tying in a complex configuration of mixture density models can be exploited by using shared codebooks for multiple lower-dimensional sub-spaces of the original feature space [57]. This approach was used successfully in [50] to compress the storage requirements of a large-vocabulary Chinese hand-written character recognition system by a factor of 10 without sacrificing recognition accuracy.

4.3.2 Model Architecture

According to the sequential structure of handwriting data the most obvious topology for hidden Markov models, as applied in HWR, is the linear architecture. Here every state is connected to itself and to its immediate successor state to the right. Note that for Arabic HWR the same holds but, as Arabic is written from right to left, here linear topologies with reversed directionality represent the methodology of choice [38]. Since larger contexts are typically not relevant for modeling handwriting the number of neighbors that are directly connected to some particular HMM state is usually restricted to more or less directly adjacent states. In order to allow for more variability in the length of the segments described by some basic model, the skipping of the immediate successor state is frequently allowed. Consequently, in this so-called Bakis topology every state has three potential successors (see Fig. 4.2). Most major recognition systems are based on either the linear or the Bakis topology (cf., e.g., [26, 33, 38–40, 45, 56]).

The number of states per character model is usually fixed according to certain heuristics. Often the average lengths of characters to be modeled (optionally

Fig. 4.2 Most common
model topologies used for
elementary units in
HMM-based writing models
(*Upper*: linear; *lower*: Bakis)

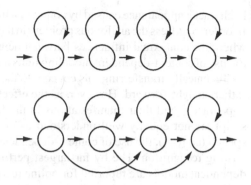

determined on outlier-reduced sample sets) in combination with the chosen model
architecture determine the number of states used (see Sect. 5). There are, however,
also approaches for model optimization, e.g., with respect to the number of states
(individually) used per character model (cf., e.g., [58–60]), that allow for minor
improvements in classification accuracy. For example, Bakis models with n states
could cover characters with a minimum length of $n/2$ frames, thereby—due to
self-transitions—not implying an upper limit for the sequence length.

According to the literature, linear (or Bakis) modeling represents the basis for the
majority of current HWR systems. However, in addition to this, certain specialized
architectures for character models have been developed. In [14] a rather complicated topology is described, which is based on eight internal states. However, the
necessity of some specialized model architecture is in this case certainly justified
by the segmentation-based nature of the overall approach. The same holds for the
"handmade" model architecture in [16]. Especially for the recognition of isolated
East Asian characters a systematic procedure for designing an optimized multi-path
character model is proposed in [61]. For signature verification in [62] a ring-topology
of HMMs is successfully applied.

For standard HMMs the duration that a model can spend in a particular state
is implicitly modeled by a geometric probability distribution. However, in some
(rare) cases it can be beneficial to explicitly model the probability of consecutively
observing some number of states in a particular state. In [54] experiments with
explicit state duration modeling for MM-based HWR are described. It is shown that
explicit state duration modeling can best be achieved using Gamma distributions.

4.3.3 Context-Dependent Models

For alphabetic scripts, as, e.g., Roman or Arabic, building writing models on the basis
of modeling units corresponding to individual characters seems a natural choice.
However, as the elementary models are trained with all samples of the respective
character not regarding how these are embedded in the context of words, variations

in character appearance caused by contextual influences can not be taken into account. In order to address the analogous problem in the field of automatic speech recognition, where the contextual influences between neighboring phones need to be modeled, the use of context-dependent modeling units has been proposed (cf. [63, pp. 95 –96]).

Technically transferring this concept to the domain of handwriting recognition is rather straight-forward. However, as the effects of contextual influence of character appearances and their manifestations in the feature representations of handwritten script are not equally well understood as those observed for phonetic contexts in speech (cf. [64]), the use of context-dependent units has had far less impact in handwriting recognition. The by far largest performance improvements using context-dependent models are reported for online recognition tasks [65–67]. In contrast, for offline recognition the effects of such model structures are usually far less pronounced [64, 68, 69]. An interesting variant of this topic appears in the context of online recognition of isolated characters in Asian scripts, as, e.g., Kanji or Chinese. There, sub-strokes are used as elementary units to build models for the quite complex character appearances (cf., e.g., [70]). Similar to context-dependent character models the necessary sub-stroke units can also be described using context-dependent models [71].

4.3.4 2D-Extensions for Offline Recognition

The predominant approach for making HMMs cope with handwriting data in the form of offline captured images is the aforementioned serialization of the images by means of the sliding window technique. Despite its popularity and its doubtless effectiveness, alternative approaches for directly dealing with two-dimensional handwriting data have also been developed. Basically, these techniques address the direct treatment of the data by the HMM without the need for explicit "conversion".

In [37] the use of planar HMMs, i.e., writing models whose outputs are also modeled using HMMs, for Arabic handwriting recognition is described. The five (horizontal) writing zones are covered by 1D-HMMs whose combined evaluation allows for directly analyzing image data without the need for explicit serialization. Alternatively, by means of the integration of Markov Random Fields (MRF) into MM-based handwriting recognition systems, handwriting images can be processed (cf., e.g., [72, 73]). Although 2D-extensions of the writing model are reasonable for certain applications explicit serialization of handwriting images is, apparently, more promising.

4.3.5 Adaptation

The ultimate goal of automatic handwriting recognition systems is their independence of any constraints regarding the handwriting analyzed. Among others this includes writer independence as well as robustness with respect to different writing styles, or lexicon changes. In order to reach this level of independence for practical applications, model adaptation techniques developed in the field of automatic speech recognition have been transferred to the problem of online and offline handwriting recognition.

Probably the first reports on the use of HMM adaptation techniques for hand-writing recognition can be found in [74, 75]. By using either maximum a-posteriori (MAP, [76]) adaptation or Maximum Likelihood Linear Regression (MLLR, cf. [77]) improvements in recognition performance are achieved. Similar experiments have also been reported in [78–82]. In [83] model adaptation is further combined with a discriminative training criterion. These research reports demonstrate that model adaptation with respect to writer changes or changes in script appearance can be realized effectively. However, the performance improvements achievable usually come at a price as the quite complicated interplay of different parameter estimation procedures used in [79] and [83] show.

4.4 The Role of Language Models

In the statistical recognition paradigm the writing model represented by the HMM needs to be complemented by the language model component for the representation of long-term sequencing constraints. As such long term constraints are not essential for all applications of HWR the use of a language model is not as widespread as in the field of automatic speech recognition. However, in recent years the application of language models for handwritten text recognition and the so-called lexicon-free recognition of virtually unlimited vocabularies have become quite popular.

4.4.1 Word-Based Language Models

In applications of handwritten text recognition where sequences of words are fed into a statistical recognizer without the prior attempt to perform a segmentation, word-based language models are used in much the same way as in automatic speech recognition. Probably the first report involving the use of statistical language models for handwritten text recognition is given in [84]. The authors investigated the relation between uni- and bi-gram language models of different perplexities in detail, and their impact on recognition quality in writer-independent experiments. In [85] a bi-gram language of similar origin is combined in different parameterizations with a writing model to create alternative recognizers. The perplexity of the model, however, is not given. The considerable performance gains to be achieved by using a bi-gram language model were confirmed by [39] for a quite similar task. Recently, a tri-gram model was used in experiments on the same database [40].

A slightly different use of language models is reported in [53]. There the primary goal is not the recognition of the written text but the classification of spontaneous handwriting obtained from survey forms into a small number of semantic classes.

Preliminary results for uni- and bi-gram models are given, which, due to the unique nature of the task, can however not be put into perspective.

Unquestionably, the most detailed account of the impact of word-based language modeling on HWR performance is given in [27]. The authors create uni-, bi-, and tri-gram language models on different text corpora and use them in recognition experiments on three different corpora of handwritten text (including a writer independent task). As expected, the use of a language model considerably improves recognition accuracy. However, it does not become completely clear why the perplexities obtained for bi-, and tri-gram models—and consequently the recognition accuracies achieved—remain relatively close in all configurations investigated.

4.4.2 Character-Based Language Models

A quite interesting method for using n-gram models in HWR is to apply them at the character level. Thus the explicit use of a lexicon can—to some degree—be avoided and recognition is performed in so-called lexicon-free mode.

Character-based language models were first proposed for the recognition of degraded machine printed documents in [48] and later applied to handwriting recognition in [86]. Experiments on a small (four writers) word-segmented database are reported for 3-, 5-, and 7-gram models including perplexities. In [87] the same methodology is applied to the problem of address recognition. Quite promising results have been obtained for back-off smoothed n-gram models up to length 7.

The lexicon-free approach has also been applied successfully to text recognition tasks, i.e., without relying on word pre-segmentation. Character tri-gram models were used in [40] whereas n-gram model lengths from 2 to 5 were investigated in [88] and later in [39].

4.4.3 Integration

Especially for the use of long-span statistical language models as presented above, the correct integration of the writing and the language model during decoding is of fundamental importance. Unfortunately, details about the solutions used can rarely be found in the literature.

In both [27] and [53] the combination of HMM and n-gram model is compiled into a combined finite state automaton usually referred to as a word network. (cf., e.g., [89, Chap. 12]).

Research groups that entered the field of HWR from the area of automatic speech recognition usually apply the same decoder as previously developed for automatic speech recognition, which is then referred to via bibliographic reference only. Thus in [86] a stack decoder and in [39] a time-synchronous decoder applying beam-search and time-based copies of search-trees is used, whereas the system described in [40] applies a two-pass decoding strategy [90].

4.5 Multi-Classifier Combination

Probably due to the growing popularity of multi-classifier systems and methods for combining classifiers, several researchers also explored such techniques in the context of MM-based offline HWR. In [55] different classifiers are derived from different feature representations. The combination of the different hypotheses obtained is then achieved by a slight variant of the ROVER framework [91], which was originally proposed in the context of automatic speech recognition. On a small (six writers) proprietary data set, significant performance improvements are reported. In [92] structurally different HMM-based classifiers are combined. Two of these follow the classical architecture and differ mainly in the type of modeling units used. The third classifier is a hybrid system combining an HMM with a multi-layer perceptron for output modeling. For the combination of results for an isolated word recognition task the best performance is reported for a method based on a neuronal network.

A rather unusual combination method is proposed in [93]. HMMs for word models are assumed to result from a concatenation of character models. Different such models are built by different training methods, namely boosting and bagging. Finally, combined models are formed by allowing the character sequences within a word model to switch freely between model variants. Results reported on a small task (only six writers) show a minor improvement which might, however, not be significant.

The multi-classifier system reported in [85] is constructed by varying the parameters for combining HMMs and n-gram models used. The combined result is then obtained by simply applying ROVER. Significant improvements are reported on a large vocabulary recognition task for a combination of 18 individual configurations.

An interesting application of a multi-classifier approach is reported in [94, 95]. The three baseline classifiers for recognition of Arabic handwriting are constructed by compensating for different slant angles during feature extraction. As only the recognition of isolated words is considered, the combination of the results can be achieved by a second classification stage which is most successfully realized as an MLP.

At a more abstract level, multi-pass recognition techniques are also related to multi-classifier approaches. As, for example, described in [18, 96, 97], MM-based HWR systems have been developed that combine the results of at least two consecutive recognition stages.

The combined use of HMMs and neuronal networks for HWR reported in [10] and refined in [11], can be considered a mixture between a multi-pass recognition and parallel classifier combination. First, HMM-based classifiers are used for character segmentation. Then NN-based character classifiers produce local recognition scores that are finally combined by a NN classifier with the scores obtained from the HMMs.

References

1. Arica N, Yarman-Vural FT (2001) An overview of character recognition focused on off-line handwriting. IEEE Trans Syst Man Cybern—Part C: Appl Rev 31(2):216–232
2. Bunke H (2003) Recognition of cursive Roman handwriting—Past, present and future. In: Proceedings of the international conference on document analysis and recognition, vol 1. Edinburgh, Scotland, pp 448–459
3. Steinherz T, Rivlin E, Intrator N (1999) Offline cursive script word recognition–A survey. Int J Document Anal Recognit 2:90–110
4. Vinciarelli A (2002) A survey on off-line cursive word recognition. Pattern Recognit 35:1433–1446
5. Lu Z, Schwartz R, Raphael C (2000) Script-independent, HMM-based text line finding for OCR. In: Proceedings of the international conference on pattern recognition, Barcelona, Spain, pp 551–554
6. Abuzaraida MA, Zeki AM, Zeki AM (2010) Segmentation techniques for online Arabic handwriting recognition: a survey. In: Proceedings of the international conference on information and communication technology for the muslim world, Jakarta, Indonesia
7. Madhvanath S, Govindaraju V (2001) The role of holistic paradigms in handwritten word recognition. IEEE Trans Pattern Anal Mach Intell 23(2):149–164
8. Arica N, Yarman-Vural FT (2000) One-dimensional representation of two-dimensional information for HMM based handwriting recognition. Pattern Recognit Lett 21:583–592
9. Arica N, Yarman-Vural FT (2002) Optical character recognition for cursive handwriting. IEEE Trans Pattern Anal Mach Intell 24(6):801–813
10. Koerich AL, Leydier Y, Sabourin R, Suen CY (2002) A hybrid large vocabulary handwritten word recognition system using neuronal networks with hidden Markov models. In: Proceedings of the international workshop on frontiers in handwriting recognition, Niagara on the Lake, Canada, pp 99–104
11. Koerich AL, Britto AS, de Oliviera LES, Sabourin R (2006) Fusing high- and low-level features for handwritten word recognition. In: Proceedings of the international workshop on frontiers in handwriting recognition, La Baule, France, pp 151–156
12. Morita M, Sabourin R, Bortolozzi F, Suen CY (2002) Segmentation and recognition of handwritten dates. In: Proceedings of the international workshop on frontiers in handwriting recognition. Niagara on the Lake, Canada, pp 105–110
13. Kundu A, Hines T, Phillips J, Huyck BD, Van Guilder LC (2007) Arabic handwriting recognition using variable duration HMM. In: Proceedings of the international conference on document analysis and recognition. vol 2. Curitiba, Brazil, pp 644–648
14. El-Yacoubi A, Gilloux M, Sabourin R, Suen CY (1999) An HMM-based approach for off-line unconstrained handwritten word modeling and recognition. IEEE Trans Pattern Anal Mach Intell 21(8):752–760
15. Grandidier F, Sabourin R, Suen CY (2003) Integration of contextual information in handwriting recognition systems. In: Proceedings of the international conference on document analysis and recognition, vol 2. Edinburgh, Scotland, pp 1252–1256
16. Morita M, El Yacoubi A, Sabourin R, Bortolozzi F, Suen CY (2001) Handwritten month word recognition on Brazilian bank cheques. In: Proceedings of the international conference on document analysis and recognition, Seattle, USA, pp 972–976
17. Tay YH, Pierre-Michel L, Khalid M, Knerr S, Virad-Gaudin C (2001) An analytical handwritten word recognition system with word-level discriminant training. In: Proceedings of the international conference on document analysis and recognition, Seattle, USA, pp 726–730
18. Britto AdS, Sabourin R, Bortolozzi F, Suen CY (2001) A two-stage HMM-based system for recognizing handwritten numeral strings. In: Proceedings of the international conference on document analysis and recognition, Seattle, USA, pp 396–400

19. Graves A, Liwicki M, Fernandez S, Bertolami R, Bunke H, Schmidhuber J (2009) A novel connectionist system for unconstrained handwriting recognition. IEEE Trans Pattern Anal Mach Intell 31(5):855–868

20. Jaeger S, Manke S, Reichert J, Waibel A (2001) Online handwriting recognition: The NPen++ recognizer. Int J Document Anal Recognit 3:169–180

21. Manke S, Finke M, Waibel A (1994) Combining bitmaps with dynamic writing information for on-line handwriting recognition. In: Proceedings of the international conference on pattern recognition, vol 2, pp 596–598

22. Schenkel M, Guyon I, Henderson D (1994) On-line cursive script recognition using time delay neural networks and hidden Markov models. In: Proceedings of the international conference on acoustics, speech, and signal processing, Adelaide, Australia, vol 2, pp 637–640

23. Dolfing JGA, Haeb-Umbach R (1997) Signal representations for Hidden Markov Model based on-line handwriting recognition. In: Proceedings of the international conference on acoustics, speech, and signal processing, Munich, Germany, vol IV, pp 3385–3388

24. El Abed H, Märgner V (2007) Comparison of different preprocessing and feature extraction methods for offline recognition of handwritten Arabic words. In: Proceedings of the international conference on document analysis and recognition, vol 2, Curitiba, Brazil, pp 974–978

25. Feng B, Ding X, Wu Y (2002) Chinese handwriting recognition using hidden Markov models. In: Proceedings of the international conference on pattern recognition, vol 3, Montréal, Canada, pp 212–215

26. Marti UV, Bunke H (2001) Using a statistical language model to improve the performance of an HMM-based cursive handwriting recognition systems. Int J Pattern Recognit Artif Intell 15(1):65–90

27. Vinciarelli A, Bengio S, Bunke H (2004) Offline recognition of unconstrained handwritten texts using HMMs and statistical language models. IEEE Trans Pattern Anal Mach Intell 26(6):709–720

28. Makhoul JI, Schwartz RM (1999) Language-independent and segmentation-free optical character recognition system and method. U.S. patent no. 5,933,525

29. Natarajan P, Lu Z, Schwartz R, Bazzi I, Makhoul J (2001) Multilingual machine printed OCR. Int J Pattern Recognit Artif Intell 15(1):43–63

30. Cho W, Lee SW, Kim JH (1995) Modeling and recognition of cursive words with hidden Markov models. Pattern Recognit 28(12):1941–1953

31. Nopsuwanchai R, Biem A, Clocksin WF (2006) Maximization of mutual information for offline Thai handwriting recognition. IEEE Trans Pattern Anal Mach Intell 28(8):1347–1351

32. Pechwitz M, Märgner V (2003) HMM based approach for handwritten Arabic word recognition using the IFN/ENIT-database. In: Proceedings of the international conference on document analysis and recognition, vol 2. Edinburgh, Scotland, pp 890–894

33. Brakensiek A, Rigoll G Handwritten address recognition using hidden Markov models. In: Dengel A, Junker M, Weisbecker A (eds) Reading and learning—adaptive content recognition, Lecture Notes in Computer Science. pp 103–122 Springer, Berlin, (2004)

34. Coetzer J, Herbst BM, du Preez JA (2006) Off-line signature verification: A comparison between human and machine performance. In: Proceedings of the international workshop on frontiers in handwriting recognition, La Baule, France, pp 481–486

35. Fink GA, Plötz T (2005) On appearance-based feature extraction methods for writer-independent handwritten text recognition. In: Proceedings of the international conference on document analysis and recognition, IEEE, vol 2. Seoul, Korea, pp 1070–1074

36. Dehghan M, Faez K, Ahmadi M, Shridhar M (2000) Off-line unconstrained Farsi handwritten word recognition using fuzzy vector quantization and hidden Markov word models. In: Proceedings of the international conference on pattern recognition, vol 2, Barcelona, Spain, pp 351–354

37. Touj SM, Ben Amara NE, Amiri H (2007) A hybrid approach for off-line Arabic handwriting recognition based on a planar hidden Markov modeling. In: Proceedings of the international conference on document analysis and recognition, vol 2. Curitiba, Brazil, pp 964–968

38. El-Hajj R, Likforman-Sulem L, Mokbel C (2005) Arabic handwriting recognition using baseline dependant features and hidden Markov modeling. In: Proceedings of the international conference on document analysis and recognition, vol 2. Seoul, Korea, pp 893–897
39. Wienecke M, Fink GA, Sagerer G (2005) Toward automatic video-based whiteboard reading. Int J Document Anal Recognit 7(2–3):188–200
40. Natarajan P, Saleem S, Prasad R, MacRostie E, Subramanian K (2004) Multi-lingual offline handwriting recognition using hidden Markov models: a script-independent approach. In: Doermann DS, Jaeger S (eds) Arabic and Chinese handwriting recognition: SACH 2006 selected papers, Lecture Notes in Computer Science. Springer, Berlin, pp 231–250
41. Lorigo LM, Govindaraju V (2006) Offline Arabic handwriting recognition: a survey. IEEE Trans Pattern Anal Mach Intell 28(5):712–724
42. Daniels, PT, Bright, W (eds) (1996) The World's writing systems. Oxford University Press, New York, USA
43. Menasri F, Vincent N, Augustin E, Cheriet M (2007) Shape-based alphabet for off-line Arabic handwriting recognition. In: Proceedings of the international conference on Document Analysis and Recognition, vol 2, Curitiba, Brazil, pp 969–973
44. Xu Q, Kim JH, Lam L, Suen CY (2002) Recognition of handwritten month words on bank cheques. In: Proceedings of the international workshop on frontiers in handwriting recognition, Niagara on the Lake, Canada, pp 111–116
45. Schambach MP (2003) Determination of the number of writing variants with an HMM based cursive word recognition system. In:Proceedings of the international conference on Document Analysis and Recognition, vol 1, Edinburgh, Scotland, pp 119–123
46. Schambach MP, Rottland J, Alary T (2008) How to convert a Latin handwriting recognition system to Arabic. In: Proceedings of the international conference on frontiers in handwriting recognition, Montréal, Canada
47. Xue H, Govindaraju V (2006) Hidden Markov models combining discrete symbols and continuous attributes in handwriting recognition. IEEE Trans Pattern Anal Mach Intell 28(3):458–462
48. Brakensiek A, Willett D, Rigoll G (2000) Improved degraded document recognition with hybrid modeling techniques and character n-grams. In: Proceedings of the international conference on Pattern Recognition, vol 4, Barcelona, Spain, pp 438–441
49. España-Boquera S, Castro-Bleda M, Gorbe-Moya J, Zamora-Martinez F (2011) Improving offline handwritten text recognition with hybrid HMM/ANN models. IEEE Trans Pattern Anal Mach Intell 33(4):767–779
50. Ge Y, Huo Q (2002) A study on the use of CDHMM for large vocabulary offline recognition of handwritten Chinese characters. In: Proceedings of the international workshop on frontiers in handwriting recognition, Niagara on the Lake, Canada, pp 334–338
51. Günter S, Bunke H (2004) HMM-based handwritten word recognition: on the optimization of the number of states, training iterations and Gaussian components. Pattern Recognit 37:2069–2079
52. Su TH, Zhang TW, Huang HJ, Zhou Y (2007) HMM-based recognizer with segmentation-free strategy for unconstrained Chinese handwriting text. In: Proceedings of the international conference on Document Analysis and Recognition, vol 1, Curitiba, Brazil, pp 133–137
53. Toselli AH, Juan A, Vidal E (2004) Spontaneous handwriting recognition and classification. In: Proceedings of the international conference on pattern recognition, vol 1, Cambridge, UK, pp 433–436
54. Benouareth A, Ennaji A, Sellami M (2006) Semi-continuous HMMs with explicit state duration applied to Arabic handwritten word recognition. In: Proceedings of the international workshop on frontiers in handwriting recognition, La Baule, France, pp 97–102
55. Brakensiek A, Rigoll G (2002) Combination of multiple classifiers for handwritten word recognition. In: Proceedings of the international workshop on frontiers in handwriting recognition, Niagara on the Lake, Canada, pp 117–122

56. Plötz T, Thurau C, Fink GA (2008) Camera-based whiteboard reading: New approaches to a challenging task. In: Proceedings of the international conference on frontiers in handwriting recognition, Montreal, Canada, pp 385–390
57. Bocchieri E, Mak BKW (2001) Subspace distribution clustering hidden Markov model. IEEE Trans Speech Audio Process 9(2):264–275
58. Geiger J, Schenk J, Wallhoff F, Rigoll G (2010) Optimizing the number of states for HMM-based on-line handwritten whiteboard recognition. In: Proceedings of the international conference on frontiers in handwriting recognition, Kolkata, India, pp 107–112
59. Günter S, Bunke H (2003) Optimizing the number of states, training iterations and Gaussians in an HMM-based handwritten word recognizer. In: Proceedings of the international conference on document analysis and recognition, vol 1. Edinburgh, Scotland, pp 472–476
60. Zimmermann M, Bunke H (2002) Hidden Markov model length optimization for handwriting recognition systems. In: Proceedings of the international workshop on frontiers in handwriting recognition, Niagara on the Lake, Canada, pp 369–374
61. Han S, Chang M, Zou Y, Chen X, Zhang D (2007) Systematic multi-path HMM topology design for online handwriting recognition of east Asian characters. In: Proceedings of the international conference on document analysis and recognition. vol 2, pp 604–608
62. Coetzer J, Herbst BM, du Preez JA (2004) Offline signature verification using the discrete Radon transform and a hidden Markov models. EURASIP J Appl Signal Process 4:559–571
63. Lee KF (1989) Automatic speech recognition: the development of the SPHINX system. Kluwer Academic Publishers, Boston
64. Fink GA, Plötz T (2007) On the use of context-dependent modelling units for HMM-based offline handwriting recognition. In: Proceedings of the international conference on document analysis and recognition, Curitiba, Brazil, pp 729–733
65. Fink GA, Vajda S, Bhattacharya U, S P, Chaudhuri BB (2010) Online Bangla word recognition using sub-stroke level features and hidden Markov models. In: Proceedings of the international conference on frontiers in handwriting recognition, Kolkata, India, pp 393–398
66. Kosmala A, Rottland J, Rigoll G (1997) Improved on-line handwriting recognition using context dependent hidden Markov models. In: Proceedings of the international conference on document analysis and recognition, vol 2. Ulm, Germany, pp 641–644
67. Rigoll G, Kosmala A, Willett D (1998) An investigation of context-dependent and hybrid modeling techniques for very large vocabulary on-line cursive handwriting recognition. In: Proceedings of the international workshop on frontiers in handwriting recognition, Taejon, Korea
68. Bianne-Bernard AL, Menasri F, Al-Haji M, Mokbel C, Kermorvant C, Likforman-Sulem L (2011) Dynamic and contextual information in HMM modeling for handwritten word recognition. IEEE Trans Pattern Anal Mach Intell (in press)
69. Saleem S, Cao H, Subramanian K, Kamali M, Prasad R, Natarajan P (2009) Improvements in BBN's HMM-based offline Arabic handwriting recognition system. In: Proceedings of the international conference on document analysis and recognition, Barcelona, Spain, pp 773–777
70. Nakai M, Akira N, Shimodaira H, Sagayama S (2001) Substroke approach to HMM-based on-line Kanji handwriting recognition. In: Proceedings of the international conference on document analysis and recognition, Seattle, USA, pp 491–495
71. Tokuno J, Inami N, Matsuda S, Nakai M, Shimodaira H, Sagayama S (2002) Context-dependent substroke model for HMM-based on-line handwriting recognition. In: Proceedings of the international conference on workshop on frontiers in handwriting recognition, Niagara on the Lake, Canada, pp 78–83
72. Choisy C (2007) Dynamic handwritten keyword spotting based on the NSHP-HMM. In: Proceedings of the international conference on document analysis and recognition, vol 1. Curitiba, Brazil, pp 242–246
73. Vajda S, Belaïd A (2005) Structural information implant in a context based segmentation-free HMM handwritten word recognition system for Latin and Bangla scripts. In: Proceedings of

the international conference on document analysis and recognition, vol 2. Seoul, Korea, pp 1126–1130

74. Brakensiek A, Kosmala A, Rigoll G (2001) Comparing adaptation techniques for on-line handwriting recognition. In: Proceedings of the international conference on document analysis and recognition, Seattle, USA, pp 486–490

75. Brakensiek A, Rottland J, Wallhoff F, Rigoll G (2001) Adaptation of an address reading system to local mail streams. In: Proceedings of the international conference on document analysis and recognition, Seattle, USA, pp 872–876

76. Gauvain JL, Lee CH (1992) MAP estimation of continuous density HMM: Theory and applications. In: Proceedings of the DARPA speech and natural language workshop, Harriman, USA

77. Leggetter CJ, Woodland PC (1995) Maximum likelihood linear regression for speaker adaptation of continuous density hidden Markov models. Comput Speech Lang 9:171–185

78. Cao H, Prasad R, Natarajan P (2010) Improvements in HMM adaptation for handwriting recognition using writer identification and duration adaptation. In: Proceedings of the international conference on frontiers in handwriting recognition, Kolkata, India, pp 154–159

79. Dreuw P, Rybach D, Gollan C, Ney H (2009) Writer adaptive training and writing variant model refinement for offline Arabic handwriting recognition. In: Proceedings of the international conference on document analysis and recognition, Barcelona, Spain, pp 21–25

80. Fink GA, Plötz T (2006) Unsupervised estimation of writing style models for improved unconstrained off-line handwriting recognition. In: Proceedings of the international conference on workshop on frontiers in handwriting ecognition, IEEE, La Baule, France

81. Liwicki M, Bunke H (2005) Enhancing training data for handwritten recognition of whiteboard notes with samples from a different database. In: Proceedings of the international conference on document analysis and recognition, vol 2. Seoul, Korea, pp 550–554

82. Vinciarelli A, Bengio S (2002) Writer adaptation techniques in off-line cursive word recognition. In: Proceedings of the international workshop on frontiers in handwriting recognition, Niagara on the Lake, Canada, pp 287–291

83. Dreuw P, Heigold G, Ney H (2009) Confidence-based discriminative training for model adaptation in offline Arabic handwriting recognition. In: Proceedings of the international conference on document analysis and recognition, Barcelona, Spain, pp 596–600

84. Marti UV, Bunke H (2001) On the influence of vocabulary size and language models in unconstrained handwritten text recognition. In: Proceedings of the international conference on document analysis and recognition, Seattle, pp 260–265

85. Bertolami R, Bunke H (2005) Multiple handwritten text line recognition systems derived from specific integration of a language model. In: Proceedings of the international conference on document analysis and recognition, vol 1, Seoul, Korea, pp 521–525

86. Brakensiek A, Rigoll G (2001) A comparison of character n-grams and dictionaries used for script recognition. In: Proceedings of the international conference on document analysis and recognition, Seattle, USA, pp 241–245

87. Brakensiek A, Rottland J, Rigoll G (2002) Handwritten address recognition with open vocabulary using character n-grams. In: Proceedings of the international workshop on frontiers in handwriting recognition, Niagara on the Lake, Canada, pp 357–362

88. Wienecke M, Fink GA, Sagerer G (2002) Experiments in unconstrained offline handwritten text recognition. In: Proceedings of the international conference on frontiers in handwriting recognition, IEEE, Ontario, Canada

89. Fink GA (2008) Markov models for pattern recognition–from theory to applications. Springer, Heidelberg

90. Austin S, Schwartz R, Placeway P (1991) The forward-backward search algorithm. In: Proceedings of the international conference on Acoustics, Speech, and Signal Processing, Toronto, Canada, pp 697–700

91. Fiscus J (1997) A post-processing system to yield reduced word error rates: Recognizer output voting error reduction. In: Furui S, Huang BH, Chu W (eds) In: Proceedings of the interna-

tional workshop on automatic speech recognition and understanding, Santa Barbara, USA, pp 352–347

92. Kermorvant C, Menasri F, Bianne A, Al-Hajj R, Mokbel C, Likforman-Sulem L (2010) The A2iA-Telecom ParisTech-UOB system for the ICDAR 2009 handwriting recognition competition. In: Proceedings of the international conference on frontiers in handwriting recognition, Kolkata, India, pp 247–252

93. Günter S, Bunke H (2002) A new combination scheme for HMM-based classifiers and its application to handwriting recognition. In: Proceedings of the international conference on pattern recognition, vol 2. Montréal, Canada, pp 332–337

94. Al-Hajj R, Mokbel C, Likforman-Sulem L (2007) Combination of HMM-based classifiers for recognition of Arabic handwritten words. In: Proceedings of the international conference on document analysis and recognition, vol 2. Curitiba, Brazil, pp 959–963

95. Al-Hajj Mohamad R, Likforman-Sulem L, Mokbel C (2009) Combining slanted-frame classifiers for improved HMM-based Arabic handwriting recognition. IEEE Trans Pattern Anal Mach Intell 31(7):1165–1177

96. Wang W, Brakensiek A, Kosmala A, Rigoll G (2001) Multi-branch and two-pass HMM modeling approaches for off-line cursive handwriting recognition. In: Proceedings of the international conference on document analysis and recognition, Seattle, USA, pp 231–235

97. Wang W, Brakensiek A, Rigoll G (2002) Combining HMM-based two-pass classifiers for off-line word recognition. In: Proceedings of the international conference on Pattern Recognition, vol 3. Montréal, Canada, pp 151–154

Chapter 5
Recognition Systems for Practical Applications

Abstract Aiming at a comprehensive overview of Markov-model based handwriting recognition this chapter focusses on the description of recognition *systems* for practical applications. After the theoretical aspects and key developments in the field have been surveyed, integration aspects and concrete evaluations of recognition capabilities are discussed. The chapter starts with a description of the most relevant datasets. As usual for all experimental science, handwriting recognition research relies on the availability of high-quality sample data for training and evaluation purposes. According to the general shift of research efforts from online to offline handwriting recognition, the majority of systems described in the current literature is dedicated to offline recognition. Reviewing the literature, we identified seven major recognition systems. We concentrated on those systems that are still being maintained and further developed. In this chapter their key features will be described and performance figures will be given.

Keywords Datasets · Organizations · Research groups · Frameworks · Toolkits · Evaluation

The theoretical foundations of Markov models are, basically, independent of their specific application domain. However, when aiming at fully functional MM-based recognition systems that can actually be used for practical tasks, domain-specific know-how is the key prerequisite for their successful application. Consequently, the majority of this kind of HWR research effort performed in the last 20+ years has been devoted to the development of techniques for the adoption of Markov models to handwriting recognition.

Aiming at a comprehensive overview of Markov-model based HWR as it is actually performed in current practical applications, in the following the focus of this book is shifted towards the description of recognition *systems*. After the theoretical aspects and key developments in the field have been surveyed, integration aspects and concrete evaluations of recognition capabilities are now discussed.

T. Plötz and G. A. Fink, *Markov Models for Handwriting Recognition*,
SpringerBriefs in Computer Science, DOI: 10.1007/978-1-4471-2188-6_5,
© Thomas Plötz 2011

Reviewing the literature, we identified seven major recognition systems. We concentrated on those systems that, according to recent publications and to the authors' best knowledge, are still being maintained and developed by the particular authors and are thus of value for the community. For most of the systems detailed descriptions exist. Furthermore, numerous refinements are often described in the particular follow-up publications. Offline recognition system represent the majority of what is described in the literature. Reasoned by the universality of the Markov model framework, a few systems have been used for both online and offline recognition. Dedicated online systems can only rarely be found in the literature and thus represent the minority of (H)MM-based HWR systems.

We begin our discussion of HWR systems with a section on data-sets. As usual for all experimental science, handwriting recognition research relies on the availability of high-quality sample data. For training and evaluating recognition systems, annotated sample data have to be recorded within the particular application domains of interest. Reasoned by the importance and practical relevance of automatic reading systems in general and of handwriting recognition systems in particular, a very active research community has been established over the years. In the past this community has devoted substantial efforts to recording and maintaining sets of a wide range of handwritten data. This comprises both online data—usually consisting of x, y, z trajectories of, for example, a stylus—and offline data, i.e., images of handwriting. Whereas a substantial number of offline HWR data-sets exists, the number of publicly available sets that cover online data is rather limited. One potential reason for this imbalance is, again, the tremendous success of commercial online handwriting recognition systems, which lets researchers focus more on offline recognition tasks.

In the 1990s the Unipen project [1] marked a major data collection endeavor in the online handwriting recognition domain. Lead by Lambert Schomaker from Nijmegen Institute for Cognition and Information in Nijmegen, Netherlands, a consortium consisting of a multitude of research institutes and about 40 companies worked on a project of data exchange and benchmarks for online handwriting recognition. Unipen stimulated substantial research efforts in the domain of online HWR and promoted the standardized evaluation of related systems, e.g., during the Unipen benchmarks. Unipen mainly focussed on isolated character recognition. In-fact, only one of the 11 benchmarks was devoted to "text" (minimally two words). More recently, the online handwriting databases collected and maintained by the University of Bern (IAM datasets, see below) have been used heavily for system development and evaluation.

Recently, considerable community efforts have been devoted to create a centralized access point to handwriting data. The technical committee "Reading Systems" (TC-11) of the International association for pattern recognition (IAPR) "is concerned with theory and application of Reading Systems".[1] On its website[2] TC-11 hosts and maintains a number of data-sets as they have been used in the literature. The motivation for making data-sets publicly available is to increase the transparency of HWR research by enabling the reproduction and cross-checking of published results.

---

[1] http://www.iapr-tc11.org

[2] http://www.iapr-tc11.org/mediawiki/index.php/Datasets_List

Furthermore, well defined benchmarks based on standardized data-sets and evaluation protocols allow for direct comparisons of the capabilities of recognition approaches.

5.1 Data-Sets

The evaluation of HWR systems is usually performed by means of practical experiments. Therefore, parameter estimation for the particular statistical models (HMMs and n-gram language models, respectively) is performed on (annotated) training data and the recognition capabilities are measured on more or less well-defined test-sets.

The description of the HWR systems, as it is given in this chapter, also includes summaries of their most important recognition results. In the following the databases that are most frequently used are briefly described. For offline experiments the documents contained by the particular databases are usually scanned with 300 dpi at a grey level resolution of 8 bit (exceptions will be denoted). For online handwriting recognition no such standard exists since the variety of data capturing technology used is based on a number of differing sensing approaches, ranging from IR/UV-based tracking of the pen to pressure sensitive surfaces. The purpose of the particular data-sets, i.e., whether they contain data for online or offline recognition (or both) will be indicated accordingly.

5.1.1 IAM-DB (Offline)

The institute of informatics and applied mathematics (IAM) at the University of Bern in Bern, Switzerland—more specifically Horst Bunke's group on Computer Vision and Artificial Intelligence—has a long history in pursuing handwriting recognition research. Apart from developing recognition systems (see Sect. 5.2.3) the group also has been involved in larger data collection projects resulting in at least three major data-sets, which are publicly available.

The IAM database (IAM-DB) represents a handwritten English sentences database for offline HWR [2]. IAM-DB consists of scanned images of handwritten English forms. The texts written to the forms originate from the LOB corpus of British English [3], a collection of texts that comprise about one million word instances. In its version 3.0, the database includes images of 1,539 forms that were produced by 657 writers, which results in a total of more than 115 k word instances. Overall a total number of 10,841 word tokens is included in the database.

5.1.2 IAM-OnDB (Online)

The IAM online handwriting database (IAM-OnDB) is the first of two major sets containing online handwriting data recorded at the University of Bern [4]. 221 persons were asked to write pre-defined texts on a whiteboard. Data recording was pursued using an e-beam^{TM} system attached to the whiteboard, which effectively tracks the pen used and provides time-stamped x, y trajectories. As for the offline version of the database, texts from the LOB corpus were written. Whereas the textual content to be written was pre-defined but no constraints regarding its appearance on the board in terms of writing style and line breaks were imposed. More than 1,700 forms, i.e., texts written on the whiteboard, were acquired resulting in approximately 13,000 isolated and labeled text lines. The database contains almost 90,000 word instances from an 11,000+ lexicon.

5.1.3 IAMonDo-DB (Online)

The second, more recent, online handwriting dataset from the University of Bern is the IAM online document database (IAMonDo-DB) [5]. In addition to handwriting—composed of texts from the Brown corpus of American English [6]—the dataset also contains "lists, tables, formulas, diagrams and drawings. Such pieces of content have been placed in arbitrary positions on each document."[3] It is, therefore, ideal for training and evaluating both handwriting recognition and layout analysis systems. 941 handwritten documents were created by 189 writers. Templates of documents were presented to the participants of the data collection endeavor, who were then asked to write and draw them onto paper. Data recording was pursued online using an Anoto[4]-like digital pen and paper system. Apart from a large number of elements that are relevant for layout analysis tasks, the database consists of approximately 70,000 words in 7,600+ text lines.

5.1.4 IAM-OnDB^{Cam} (offline)

This set of images corresponds to a side-product of the IAM online handwriting database (IAM-OnDB, see above) captured for whiteboard reading applications. It consists of color images of whiteboard texts that have been taken with a digital camera with a resolution of $3,264 \times 2,448$ pixels each. The database contains 491 documents written by 62 subjects. In total the database comprises a dictionary of 11,059 words. Unfortunately, unlike the other IAM databases this data is not yet publicly available.

5.1.5 IFN/ENIT (Offline)

The IFN/ENIT database represents a standardized set of handwritten Arabic town/ village names [7]. It consists of scanned forms produced by more than 400 writers

---

[3] iapr-tc11.org/mediawiki/index.php/IAM_Online_Document_Database_(IAMonDo-database)
[4] http://www.anoto.com

with about 26,400 city names containing 210 k+ characters. In addition to the images and their annotation, further information as for example the correct baseline of the cropped and pre-processed words are also provided.

5.1.6 RIMES (Offline)

Addressing the recognition and indexing of handwritten letters the French RIMES project (Reconnaissance et Indexation de données Manuscrites et de fac sim-ilÉS/Recognition and Indexing of handwritten documents and faxes) collected a large amount of data suitable for training and evaluating offline handwriting recognizers [8, 9]. In its original version RIMES consists of scanned images of more than 5,600 letters written by 1,300+ persons. Given that every letter consists of multiple pages, RIMES totals to almost 13,000 images of handwritten text. All letters were written in French only constrained by the general topic (chosen from one of nine pre-defined ones). Writers were asked to compose a letter addressing the particularly chosen topic using their own words. Furthermore, no layout restrictions were given, which results in very challenging tasks for both layout analysis and actual handwriting recognition. The RIMES consortium also organizes competitions on the dataset—2009 and 2011 in conjunction with ICDAR (Int. Conference on Document Analysis and Recognition) [10]. The most realistic tasks of recognizing words (rather than characters) using RIMES are based on lexicons containing either 100 (WR_100) or 1,636 (WR_1636) words.

5.2 Systems

According to the reviewed literature and to the criteria for selection as defined above, seven major Markov-model based HWR systems are considered for this book. In the following their key features and recognition results are described.

5.2.1 BBN

BBN technologies, Cambridge, USA, can be considered as one of the pioneers in transferring Markov-model based techniques from the domain of automatic speech recognition to the field of optical character recognition. Since the mid-1990s BBN worked extensively on various aspects of statistical modeling for optical character recognition (cf., e.g., [11]). BBN's recognition framework is based on the BYBLOS engine, which was originally developed for automatic speech recognition purposes (cf., e.g., [12] for a system description). Recently, BBN has successfully applied its OCR framework to the recognition of handwritten texts in different scripts [13].

Although BBN as a company mainly addresses commercial applications which usually implies certain non-disclosure of technical details, a surprisingly large number of publications exists that very thoroughly describe the recognition system(s).

The BBN handwriting recognition system follows the classical architecture of Markov model based recognizers for general sequential data. It integrates both HMMs and statistical n-gram language models. Apparently the BBN systems, which include both OCR and handwriting recognition utilizing Markov models, aim at universal applicability without language or script dependent restrictions. As an example, the OCR system has already been used for the recognition of numerous script types even including such "exotic" languages as Pashto (main language in Afghanistan) [14]. In the same way multi-linguality is addressed by BBN's research activities in Markov-model based handwriting recognition.

The primary domain of BYBLOS-based frameworks is offline recognition. The offline HWR system includes modules for complete document layout analysis that segments each input image into single column text zones. After normalization (de-skewing and line finding, plus some preliminary—according to [13]—slant correction) the latter represents the input for the recognition system. Serialization is performed using the sliding window technique where overlapping frames are extracted for every line of text. Thereby, the height of the analysis windows equals to the height of the particular line, the width is 1/15 of the height and adjacent frames overlap by 2/3 of window width. In these frames "percentile features" [11, 15] are calculated on binarized pixels. The blackness of a frame is integrated from top to bottom. After normalizing by the sum of black pixels a monotonically increasing function encodes the amount of blackness up to any particular position within the frame. By sampling the function equidistantly, 20 features are calculated. In addition to this, horizontal and vertical derivatives, respectively, complement the feature vectors. Together with angle and correlation features (ten each) that are calculated from scatter plots of the text pixels, 80-dimensional vectors are extracted for every frame. In the description of their OCR system [11], which represents the origin of the BBN HWR system, the authors describe 80 components. However, for the HWR system in [13] 81 features are mentioned. Unfortunately, it remains unclear how the missing component is calculated. The resulting 81-dimensional feature vectors are then reduced to 15 dimensions by applying Linear Discriminant Analysis (LDA).

The BBN recognizer uses tied-mixture character HMMs as elementary writing models with 14-state Bakis topology. Different variants of mixture tying (classical global tied mixtures over all states, character tied mixtures where Gaussians are shared by states of single characters, and some mixture form of both types—state tied mixtures with a total of approximately 150 k Gaussians) are integrated for most effective exploitation of sample data for model estimation. The latter is performed using classical Baum-Welch training whereas the recognition itself is a two-pass beam-search process combining a fast forward match with a more detailed backward search [16]. Optionally, a lexicon is used during recognition, and statistical n-gram language models (word-based tri-grams) are integrated.

Apparently it is especially the large number of mixtures, which are used for output modeling, that enables truly multi-lingual handwriting recognition. Experimental evaluations have been described that address the recognition of English, Arabic, and Chinese script [13]. It needs to be mentioned that, generally, very detailed descriptions of the BBN recognizer's configuration for the particular experimental evaluations are given. For the first set of experiments the IAM-DB is used. By means of a tri-gram language model word error rates of approximately 40% have been achieved. Experiments for Chinese HWR have been conducted, for example, on the ETL9B dataset (200 instances each of 71 Hiragana and 2,965 Kanji characters—in total 3,036 unique characters). Here character-based error rates of approximately 17% were reported. Finally, the system has been evaluated on the IFN/ENIT database. Word error rates of 10.6% indicate the suitability of the BBN recognition system also for Arabic.

5.2.2 CENPARMI

Document analysis in general represents one of the major working fields of the research group of Ching Suen at the centre for pattern recognition and machine intelligence (CENPARMI) at Concordia University, Montréal, Canada including associated scientists from other institutions. Among others their activities are focused on HMM-based offline handwriting recognition. Over the years a recognition system has been developed that is successfully being used for various applications including signature verification, postal address reading, recognition of (Brazilian) bank cheques and so forth. A general system description has been published in [17]. Additionally, numerous papers addressing applications and enhancements of the basic system exist (cf., e.g., [18–20]). The base system was also used for hybrid recognition approaches or for classifier ensembles [19, 21].

The CENPARMI system for Markov-model based offline HWR differs from most of related systems in certain aspects. First, recognition relies on explicit segmentation of extracted words into (pseudo-) characters. Second, compared to other approaches, a radically differing strategy regarding feature extraction is pursued. According to El-Yacoubi et al. "lexicon-driven word recognition approaches do not require features to be very discriminative at the character or pseudo character level because other information, such as context [. . .], word length, etc., are available and permit high discrimination of words. Thus, [they] consider features at the segment level with the aim of clustering letters into classes" [17]. Furthermore, the CENPARMI system is based on discrete hidden Markov models using outputs calculated on string encodings of different feature sets.

After preprocessing word images by applying skew compensation, lower case letter area (upper-baseline) normalization, character slant correction, and smoothing, an explicit segmentation of the input data is computed. The procedure explicitly performs over-segmentation by generating a high number of possible segmentation points (SP) that sub-divide words into units that not necessarily correspond to actual characters but to some smaller portions. In this way several segmentation options are offered, the best ones to be validated during recognition. At every segmentation point the neighborhood is divided into writing zones that represent small analysis windows centered at the particular SP. Based on this, three different sets of features are calculated. The first set comprises global features (loops, ascenders, and descenders). For the second set of features bidimensional contour transition histograms of each segment in the horizontal and vertical directions are analyzed and certain statistics are derived that serve as discrete feature values (from a set of 14 symbols). Furthermore, segmentation features that reflect the way segments are linked together are considered. Optionally, an LDA transformation is applied to the resulting feature vectors aiming at the introduction of "class information during feature extraction" [18].

CENPARMI's writing models (HMMs) are based on graphemes as modeling units. A special model topology has been developed that consists of eight segment specific states and a rather complicated transition scheme. The rationale is to explicitly map the over-, under-, or correct segmentation of a letter to the model architecture. Additionally, the recognizer uses separate space models with modified linear left-to-right architecture without self transitions. Parameter estimation is performed using a slightly modified version of Baum-Welch training. Recognition itself is performed using a rather complex decoding procedure that apparently allows an implicit detection of the writing style (no further details given).

Since the CENPARMI recognizer together with variants and enhancements of the base system has been used for various application domains the results reported for experimental evaluations of its recognition capabilities are rather diverse. Addressing postal address reading experiments in recognizing unconstrainedly handwritten French city names were performed on proprietary data. Depending on the lexicon size (varying from 10 to 1,000) results between almost perfect recognition and approximately 12% word error rate have been reported for test sets containing between 4 and 11 k images [17, 18]. For the analysis of bank cheques handwritten month words, i.e., a lexicon of 12 entries, are recognized. Here recognition results of about 10% word error rate have been achieved for a set of 402 test images 62.

5.2.3 IAM

The group of Horst Bunke at the institute of informatics and applied mathematics (IAM) at the University of Bern, Bern, Switzerland can without doubt be called one of the most productive teams with substantial influence on general research in handwriting recognition. In fact one of the earliest papers on Markov-model based recognition of unconstrained cursive script, i.e., handwriting, was published by them already in 1995 [22]. Over the years numerous scientists affiliated or associated to this group (including the group at the swiss IDIAP institute) have contributed to the research field of (Markov-model based) handwriting recognition. Consequently, today IAM maintains mature handwriting recognition systems, which have successfully been applied to both online and offline recognition tasks.

The IAM system for offline reading of unconstrained handwritten pages has, for example, been described in detail in [23, 24]. Additionally, a multitude of refinements, enhancements, and specialties have been described in numerous papers published in the last years. Basically, the system follows the classical architecture of a Markov-model based recognition system as summarized in Chap. 2. Handwritten documents are pre-segmented regarding single text lines, which are then fed into the recognition system that proceeds in a segmentation-free manner, i.e., not relying on further segmentation. The IAM system integrates continuous HMMs as writing models and statistical n-grams as language models. The first step in the processing chain comprises suitable pre-processing that addresses skew and slant correction, text line normalization and horizontal scaling.

For feature extraction, text line images are serialized by means of a sliding window technique. Thereby the analysis window, that is moved from left to right along the text line, is one column wide, i.e., there is no overlap between consecutive frames. The height of the sliding window is identical to the text line's height. For every frame nine local geometrical features are computed. On the one hand these features cover the characteristics of the analysis window from a global point of view (weight of the window, center of gravity and so forth). On the other hand the features also describe details about the writing itself by considering positions and orientations of contours and certain pixel statistics. Note that variants of the feature extraction process have been described where only local grid-based pixel counts were used [24, 25]. The IAM system is based on character models with linear topology that each consist of a fixed number of 14 states (empirically found) with continuous outputs. Identical models are used for capital and lower case letters. Word models are obtained by simple concatenation of character models. Parameter estimation is performed using Baum-Welch training, and for recognition, Viterbi decoding is applied. The IAM system also integrates statistical n-gram language models (up to tri-grams), which are estimated using discounting and backing-off.

The IAM offline recognizer also has been used for whiteboard reading using the e-beam^{TM} system, i.e., for online recognition [26]. The aforementioned offline recognition framework has been applied "as is" to handwriting data, which have been acquired online by tracking the pen used. In order to make the offline recognition framework applicable to online data specialized pre-processing has been applied for de-noising the recorded trajectories by eliminating stroke outliers. Subsequently, the online trajectories are converted into offline images, thereby mimicking the characteristics of the IAM (offline) database. This conversion procedure consists of a sequence of basic image processing steps (connection of consecutive points, dilation of resulting strokes to fixed width of eight pixels, and gradient-like coloring of the strokes).

In addition to the offline HWR system used for both online and offline application, IAM has also developed a dedicated online recognizer based on Markov models, which has been used heavily for whiteboard reading (cf., e.g., [27]). Instead of converting online data into offline images and then using an offline recognizer, the IAM online recognition system treats online data directly. The pre-processing stage de-noises, and normalizes the x, y-trajectory data regarding slant, and skew, thereby operating locally on automatically extracted consecutive chunks, e.g., words. After re-sampling, delayed strokes are removed using a threshold based approach. For subsequent feature extraction the baseline and the corpus line are estimated and, finally, the width of the characters is normalized to a fixed value. The IAM online recognizer employs heuristic features for obtaining an informative representation of the input data. First, for every trajectory point a number of local features are derived, incl. pen-up/pen-down classification, hat feature (indicator for delayed stroke removal), speed, x and y coordinates, writing direction, curvature, vicinity -aspect/ -slope/ -curliness/ -linearity. These online features are then combined with a second class of features, which are computed using "a two-dimensional matrix representing the offline version of the data" [27]. The latter consist of a number of ascender/descender pixels, and a 3×3 context map.

Similar to the offline system, modeling for the online recognizer is based on character models (continuous HMM) and n-gram based language models. The original system description mentions the use of bi-gram language models [27]. HMMs exhibit linear model topology with Gaussian mixture densities (up to 36 components) for observation modeling. Model training is pursued using standard Baum-Welch training and for recognition Viterbi decoding is used. In addition to the exclusive use of either online or offline IAM systems, more recently combinations of both have been used for both online and offline recognition experiments ([28], further generalized in [29]).

The effectiveness of the overall IAM systems as well as of its recent enhancements is usually documented by the results of experimental evaluations based on the IAM databases. Depending on the actual configuration of the particular experiments and the recognizer used, for the offline case word error rates between 37.3% [30] and approximately 53% [24] have been achieved on IAM-DB. Word error rates of the offline system for IAM-OnDB tasks vary between 38.6% [28] and 42.7% [29]. The online IAM recognition system achieves word error rates of 34.8% [28]. So far, no realistic HMM-based results have been published for the—rather new—IAM-OnDo database.

5.2.4 RWTH

The research group "Human language technology and pattern recognition" led by Hermann Ney at the RWTH Aachen University in Aachen, Germany, has a long history of successful research and a strong reputation in the fields of statistical pattern recognition in general, and natural language processing in particular. With its origins lying at Philips Research laboratories, the RWTH automatic speech recognition (ASR) system can be considered as one of the most advanced recognition framework in the field [31]. It's core is largely based on Markovian models. Recently the RWTH ASR system has become open source software. The toolkit represents a valuable resource for researchers in the field of Markov model based pattern recognition in general [32].

Whereas the main focus of the group's scientific activities still lies on speech recognition and natural language processing, in the recent past considerable efforts have been devoted to Markov model based optical character recognition including processing cursive script.[5] The group mainly works on Arabic OCR [33, 34] and on Arabic HWR [34, 35]. The system has also been adapted to French HWR [36] and to English HWR [37]. Without doubt the RWTH recognition framework can thus be considered as a system that copes universally with alphabetic scripts. Both the OCR and the handwriting recognition systems are based on the RWTH ASR toolkit, which consists of (i) a signal processing module—the so-called "Flow"—that is tailored for processing raw sensor data including feature extraction, (ii) a modeling component (hidden Markov models including (C)MLLR based adaptation [38, 39]), (iii) language models, (iv) a decoder optimized for large vocabularies, and (v) a finite state automata module.

Aachen's OCR and handwriting recognition systems are used for offline recognition tasks. Images of machine printed or handwritten script are transformed into a sequential representation using the standard sliding window approach. Frames with a width of seven pixels are extracted at every position of—presumably (no details given)—line images. For Arabic recognition no specific pre-processing is applied as —according to the authors [37]— it does not have any positive effect on the performance of the system. The Roman script recognizer (for English, and French) utilizes a standard suite of pre-processing procedures including color/gray value normalization, de-slanting, and size-normalization (height). For all systems appearance-based features are extracted per frame by combining the raw pixel values of the particular analysis window with its spatial, horizontal derivatives (frame-related). By applying a Principal Component Analysis (PCA) the dimension of the feature vectors is reduced to a reasonable, i.e., most informative sub-set.

Character models are initialized with a left-right topology and three states each. Continuous feature space modeling is employed, i.e., state-specific Gaussians with a globally pooled covariance matrix are used. Given the sometimes significant variance of characters' length (especially in Arabic) subsequently an automatic model-length adaptation is applied. Thereby the number of states is determined for every character HMM using a heuristic scaling approach [40]. As a specialty for Arabic OCR and HWR, explicit models are derived for "between word whitespaces" and for "within word whitespaces" [33], and integrated into the recognition lexicon.

Model training using the RWTH framework can be done in the conventional way, i.e., by means of the standard Baum-Welch optimization procedure. Additionally the Aachen recognizers can also be trained using either constrained maximum likelihood linear regression based writer adaptive training (CMLLR-WAT), or by means of discriminative training using a modified maximum mutual information criterion (M-MMI). The former refers to writer adaptation of a writer-independent recognition system using MLLR (cf. Sect. 4.3.5) thereby employing a global regression matrix for the adaptation of both the GMM mean and variance. The latter corresponds to margin-based HMM training, which optimizes the margin between the particularly

---

[5] www-i6.informatik.rwth-aachen.de/rwth-ocr/

modeled classes ("margin posterior" weights [36]) rather than maximizing their likelihoods. The optimization criterion used (M-MMI) enhances the standard maximum mutual information criterion by integrating adjustable margin offsets (comparable to slack variables in support vector machine training, cf., e.g., [41]). M-MMI based training is a very powerful procedure, which improves recognition capabilities across domain boundaries [36].

The concept of model adaptation, as it is used for the training procedure, is also employed for model evaluation in the recognition phase (in addition to standard single-pass Viterbi decoding). Since all variants of MLLR-based model adaptation require label information, i.e., the transcription of the input data, a two-pass decoding procedure is necessary. In the first pass a standard Viterbi decoder determines a—not necessarily correct but most likely reasonable—transcription of the input data. Then, in the second stage, the original recognition system is re-trained either using the standard ML procedure or the discriminative margin-based training using M-MMI. The resulting adapted system is then used in the second pass to provide the final transcription of the input data. This two-pass decoding is unique in the Markov model based document processing domain. Comparable approaches have, however, also been used for adaptive speech recognition (cf., e.g., [42–44]).

The RWTH handwriting recognition system has been systematically evaluated on Arabic recognition tasks based on the IFN/Enit database. Recently, the framework has also been tested on the English IAM-DB and preliminary results have been reported for evaluations based on the French RIMES database (for dataset descriptions cf. Sect. 5.1). The best results reported for the ICDAR 2005 Arabic HWR competition setup (training: set a/b/c/d; test: set e) correspond to a word error rate of 14.6%—achieved with two-phase decoding and M-MMI discriminative training with confidence adaptation [36, 37]. As a baseline the RWTH recognizer based on standard ML training with fixed model length and single-pass decoding achieved 21.9% word error rate. Automatic model length estimation significantly reduces the classification error (16.8%), whereas the impact of standard discriminative training (MMI) is not as substantial (16.4%). The introduction of explicit whitespace models also has a significant impact on the classification accuracy of the Arabic HWR system. Word error rate reductions of approximately 25% can be achieved when using within-word and between-word whitespace models. Comparably promising results have been reported for IAM-DB based recognition tasks. Achieving a word error rate of 29.2% on the IAM-DB evaluation set [34] renders the RWTH system one of the most effective Markov model based (offline) handwriting recognition systems.

5.2.5 SIEMENS

The primary field of activity of the department of logistics and assembly systems—postal automation—at Siemens AG in Konstanz, Germany is address reading. Most notably automatic offline recognition systems for mail sorting as applied by major postal companies are being developed. The beginnings of the recognition system lie in developments that have been pursued already in the early 1990s—at this time at Daimler-Benz research center in Ulm, Germany [45, 46]. It evolved from a framework that had originally been developed for automatic speech recognition. Recently the system, that is created to analyze Roman script, has even been used for Arabic handwriting recognition—requiring minor modifications only [47]. Since Siemens mainly addresses commercial applications, not all details regarding the recognizer have been published, some developments might even have been patented. However, in various papers the key components of the system are described, which provides an overview of the contributions.

The Markov-model based address reading system of Siemens is applied to those automatically extracted portions of some scanned image that are relevant for mail routing (zip code, city, street and so on). Prior to actual recognition, shear angle, rotation, and stroke width and size, respectively, are normalized using (undocumented) standard procedures. Furthermore, sceletonization is applied. Handwriting is modeled by means of semi-continuous (tied mixture) hidden Markov models with full covariance matrices. The script model of the Siemens system is defined by a set of graphemes, namely letters, numbers and special characters. Variants of these graphemes—allographs—then represent the final modeling units for character HMMs that are composed to word-HMMs. The character models consists of various "paths" that can also be dynamically adapted during training. All paths are jointly followed by an optional pause state. Apparently, the number of states per character model is somehow determined automatically (no details given). The models exhibit the classical linear left-to-right topology for Roman script, and right-to-left model architecture for Arabic, respectively.

The Siemens recognizer uses the standard sliding window approach for serialization of the two-dimensional image data. The concrete parametrization of the procedure has, however, only been documented for the most recent developments at Siemens towards offline HWR for Arabic scripts [47] and it can be assumed that the parameters for the analysis of roman script are comparable. A window width of 11 pixels together with an overlap of two thirds between adjacent frames seems to be optimal. Thereby, the height of the analyzed text lines determines the vertical size of the sliding window. Feature extraction is based on the analysis of binary connected components (BCC)—black or white contour-polygons, the surrounding rectangle, and a reference to inner context areas—that are extracted on normalized and approximated word skeletons. Frames are divided into five horizontal zones where geometric features are calculated that mainly describe upstrokes and cross-lines. Additionally, curves, strokes, and cusps are described by the 20-dimensional features used [45]. In some publications an LDA-transformation is applied but, unfortunately, no further details are given.

In postal address reading the variability of putative addresses is extremely large. For practical applications of such an automatic recognition system very large vocabularies that typically contain more than 20 k words need to be considered. Efficient recognition, therefore, requires sophisticated model decoding techniques. Among others a two-stage decoding strategy was developed for the Siemens system [48]. In the first phase lexicon-free recognition is performed that produces sequences of characters. Following this, a breadth-first search on a lexicon tree including pruning is performed. It operates on intermediate results of the first step to estimate likelihoods for character paths. The latter corresponds to an effective restriction of character sequences apart from the popular use of statistical n-gram language models.

Because of its commercial background, most of the experiments performed to evaluate the recognition capabilities of the Siemens system are based on proprietary data from the company. Here, for example, word error rates for city name recognition between 6% and 12% (depending on the lexicon size of either 1,000 or 100 city names) on address reading tasks with more than 1,000 images have been achieved [48]. Since these data-sets are not publicly available, direct comparisons to other recognition systems are difficult to perform. However, since the Siemens system won the ICDAR 2007 Arabic HWR competition [49], the recognition capabilities of the system can also be compared more objectively. On the IFN/ENIT database of Tunisian city names the system achieved approximately 12% word error rate [47].

5.2.6 TPar/UoB

Another Markov-model based offline HWR system is being developed and maintained by a group of researchers around Laurence Likforman-Sulem at Telecom Paris-Tech (former GET-Ecole Nationale Supérieure des Télécommunications/TSI), Paris, France, and the University of Balamand, Faculty of engineering, Tripoli, Lebanon, respectively. The TPar/UoB system has been applied to Arabic, French and English handwriting recognition tasks. The superior recognition capabilities of the Arabic recognizer—in its state at that time [50]—were impressively demonstrated when it has won the ICDAR 2005 Arabic HWR competition [51]. In its most recent version the recognizer also achieves very competitive results on both the French 2009 RIMES benchmark and on the English IAM database [52].

The handwriting recognition system is derived from a general purpose HMM toolkit that was originally developed for speech recognition applications. A most recent description of the TPar/UoB system can be found in Al-Hajj Mohamad [53]. The basic system has been enhanced towards a hybrid recognition approach, i.e., utilizing multiple classifier combination techniques (cf. also [54]) and applying context-dependent character modeling based on decision trees [52]. The recognition system uses character-based HMMs that are concatenated to word models, which are evaluated in parallel. No further restrictions (like, for example, language models) are applied to the hypotheses generated. In contrast to earlier versions the TPar/UoB recognition system now also applies standard pre-processing, i.e., de-slanting and baseline correction (both based on Vinciarelli and Luettin [55]).

Input images are serialized using a standard sliding window technique. Further details regarding the concrete parametrization are not given. For Arabic script processing the analysis window is shifted along the word image from right to left, whereas for recognizing French handwriting the standard left-to-right procedure is applied. At every position vertical zones are created using the lower and upper baselines as previously extracted. Thereby, the middle zone does not contain ascenders and descenders, whereas in the remaining zones ascenders and descenders can be found, respectively [50]. For every frame 24-dimensional feature vectors are extracted. They consist of distribution features that are based on foreground pixel densities, one derivative feature, and concavity features. The competitive results for different languages gives evidence that the features can universally be used for any script, which can be decomposed into the aforementioned three zones.

The original Arabic recognizer modeled characters in their particular context variations (159 models in total). Every model contains four states and a mixture of three Gaussians (presumably with full covariances) for output modeling. Although it is not explicitly denoted as such, the model topology of the HMMs corresponds to a (1D) Bakis right-to-left architecture. More recently, context-dependent modeling has been introduced [52], which results in a much larger number of base models. By means of a decision tree based clustering procedure the set of—hardly trainable—context-dependent models is reduced to a reasonable set. Parameter estimation is performed using a segmental version of the standard EM algorithm. In this training procedure, which is commonly known as Viterbi training (for details cf., e.g., [56, p. 80f]), the parameter estimation is based on the most probable state sequence. Aiming for increased robustness against inclination, overlap and shifted positions of diacritical marks a combination of three homogeneous HMM-based classifiers has been proposed that all have the same topology as described here and differ only in the orientation of the sliding window [57]. Alternatively, the HMM-based recognition framework is combined with a Neural Network classifier, which post-processes the recognition hypotheses.

For the evaluation of the recognition capabilities of the TPar/UoB systems, results of recognition experiments on the IFN/ENIT database have been reported. By means of the recognition framework word error rates of approximately 13% have been achieved. The hybrid, context-dependent recognition system achieves error-rates of 21.9% on IAM, and 14.7% on RIMES (WL_1636), which both is very competitive [52].

5.2.7 TUDo

At TU Dortmund University (TUDo) in Dortmund, Germany, research in automatic offline handwriting recognition is pursued with special emphasis on camera-based approaches (cf. [58]). At the maintainers' former affiliation, Bielefeld University, Bielefeld, Germany, considerable effort was already devoted to MM-based handwriting recognition (cf., e.g., [59]) addressing for the first time the task of automatic whiteboard reading using a camera-based approach [60]. The HWR system is based on a general Markov model toolkit (ESMERALDA[6] [61]), which has originally been developed for automatic speech recognition purposes.

---

[6] http://sourceforge.net/projects/esmeralda

The general task considered by the TUDo system is writer-independent offline recognition of handwritten texts. Therefore, an integrated recognition framework is being developed, which quite closely follows the general architecture for MM-based handwriting recognizers. It uses semi-continuous HMMs as writing models and statistical n-gram models as language models. In order to allow for its application to "real-world" scenarios like the aforementioned camera-based whiteboard reading task, the TUDo system includes a text-detection module that extracts lines of text from image data. Prior to the actual recognition stage, standard pre-processing operations are applied (skew, slant and size normalization). For linearization of the two-dimensional handwriting data a sliding window approach is applied to normalized text lines. They are subdivided into a sequence of overlapping stripes of eight pixels width (overlapping each other by 75%) and the height of the line. For each of these frames a set of nine geometric features that describe the coarse shape of the writing within the local analysis window plus their first derivatives are computed. The resulting feature vectors are fed into the recognition system, which consists of word models that are built by concatenation of separate models for upper and lower case letters plus numerals, and punctuation symbols (75 in total). All models have Bakis topology and share a codebook of 1.5 k Gaussians with diagonal covariance matrices. The number of model states is automatically determined depending on the length of the respective unit in the training material (30 on average). Parameter estimation is performed using standard Baum-Welch training. Plausible word sequences, determined by the HMM decoding process (Viterbi), are restricted by word based statistical n-gram models that are estimated by applying absolute discounting and backing-off.

For the judgment of the overall recognition capabilities of the TUDo system word error rates obtained in experimental evaluations have been reported in various publications (cf., e.g., [58–60]). The basis for these experiments are either images of the IAM-DB or those from the IAM-OnDB^{Cam}. For the first task word error rates of 28.9% were reported (perplexity of bi-gram used is 645) and for the whiteboard images of IAM-OnDB 39.8% error rate are achieved (perplexity of the bi-gram used is 310).

References

1. Guyon I, Schomaker L, Plamondon R, Liberman M, Janet S (1994) UNIPEN project of on-line data exchange and recognizer benchmarks. In: Proceedings of the international conference on pattern recognition, Jerusalem, Israel, pp 29–33
2. Marti UV, Bunke H (2002) The IAM-database: An English sentence database for offline handwriting recognition. Int J Doc Anal Recogn 5(1):39–46
3. Johansson S, Leech G, Goodluck H (1978) Manual of information to accompany the Lancaster-Oslo/Bergen corpus of British English, for use with digital computers. Technical report, Department of English, University of Oslo, Norway

4. Liwicki M, Bunke H (2005) IAM-OnDB—An on-line English sentence database acquired from handwritten text on a whiteboard. In: Proceedings of the international conference on document analysis and recognition, Seoul, Korea, vol 2, pp 956–961

5. Indermühle E, Liwicki M, Bunke H (2010) IAMonDo-database: an online handwritten document database with non-uniform contents. In: Proceedings of the international workshop on document analysis systems, Boston, USA, pp 97–104

6. Francis WN, Kucera H (1964, 1971, 1979) A standard corpus of present-day edited American English, for use with digital computers (Brown). Technical report, Brown University, Providence, Rhode Island, USA

7. Pechwitz M, Maddouri SS, Märgner V, Ellouze N, Amiri H (2002) IFN/ENIT-database of handwritten arabic words. In: Proceedings of the seventh colloque international Francophone sur l'Ecrit et le document, Hammamet, Tunisia

8. Augustin E, Carré M, Grosicki E, Brodin JM, Geoffrois E, Preteux F (2006) RIMES evaluation campaign for handwritten mail processing. In: Proceedings of the international workshop on frontiers in handwriting recognition, La Baule, France, pp 231–235

9. Augustin E, Carré M, Grosicki E, Brodin JM, Geoffrois E, Prêteux F (2008) RIMES evaluation campaign for handwritten mail processing. In: Proceedings of the international conference on frontiers in handwriting recognition, Montréal, Canada

10. Grosicki E, Carré M, Brodin JM, Geoffrois E (2009) Results of the second RIMES evaluation campaign for handwritten mail processing. In: Proceedings of the international conference on document analysis and recognition, Barcelona, Spain

11. Natarajan P, Lu Z, Schwartz R, Bazzi I, Makhoul J (2001) Multilingual machine printed OCR. Int J Pattern Recogn Artif Intell 15(1):43–63

12. Colthurst T, Kimball O, Richardson F, Shu H, Wooters C, Iyer R, Gish H (2000) The 2000 BBN Byblos LVCSR system. In: 2000 speech transcription workshop, Maryland, USA

13. Natarajan P, Saleem S, Prasad R, MacRostie E, Subramanian K (2008) Multi-lingual offline handwriting recognition using hidden Markov models: A script-independent approach. In: Doermann DS, Jaeger S (eds) Arabic and chinese handwriting recognition: SACH 2006 selected papers, Lecture notes in computer science, vol 4768, Springer, Berlin Heidelberg, pp 231–250

14. Decerbo M, MacRostie E, Natarajan P (2004) The BBN Byblos Pashto OCR system. In: Proceedings of the first ACM workshop on hardcopy document processing, Washington, DC, USA, pp 29–32

15. Makhoul JI, Schwartz RM (1999) Language-independent and segmentation-free optical character recognition system and method. U.S. patent no. 5,933,525

16. Austin S, Schwartz R, Placeway P (1991) The forward-backward search algorithm. In: Proceedings of the international conference on acoustics, speech, and signal processing, Toronto, Canada, pp 697–700

17. El-Yacoubi A, Gilloux M, Sabourin R, Suen CY (1999) An HMM-based approach for off-line unconstrained handwritten word modeling and recognition. IEEE Trans Pattern Anal Mach Intell 21(8):752–760

18. Grandidier F, Sabourin R, Suen CY (2003) Integration of contextual information in handwriting recognition systems. In: Proceedings of the international conference on document analysis and recognition, Edinburgh, Scotland, vol 2, pp 1252–1256

19. Koerich AL, Leydier Y, Sabourin R, Suen CY (2002) A hybrid large vocabulary handwritten word recognition system using neuronal networks with hidden Markov models. In: Proceedings of the international workshop on frontiers in handwriting recognition, Niagara on the Lake, Canada, pp 99–104

20. Koerich AL, Britto AS, de Oliviera LES, Sabourin R (2006) Fusing high- and low-level features for handwritten word recognition. In: Proceedings of the international workshop on frontiers in handwriting recognition, La Baule, France, pp 151–156

21. Ko AHR, Sabourin R, de Souza Britto A Jr (2009) Ensemble of HMM classifiers based on the clustering validity index for a handwritten numeral recognizer. Pattern Anal Appl J 12(1):21–35

22. Bunke H, Roth M, Schukat-Talamazzini EG (1995) Off-line cursive handwriting recognition using hidden Markov models. Pattern Recogn 9(9):1399–1413
23. Marti UV, Bunke H (2001) Using a statistical language model to improve the performance of an HMM-based cursive handwriting recognition systems. Int J Pattern Recogn Artif Intell 15(1):65–90
24. Vinciarelli A, Bengio S, Bunke H (2004) Offline recognition of unconstrained handwritten texts using HMMs and statistical language models. IEEE Trans Pattern Anal Mach Intell 26(6):709–720
25. Vinciarelli A, Luettin J (2000) Off-line cursive script recognition based on continuous density HMM. In: Proceedings of the international workshop on frontiers in handwriting recognition, Amsterdam, The Netherlands, pp 493–498
26. Liwicki M, Bunke H (2005) Handwriting recognition of whiteboard notes. In: Proceedings of the twelveth conference of the international graphonomics society, Salerno, Italy, pp 118–122
27. Liwicki M, Bunke H (2006) HMM-based on-line recognition of handwritten whiteboard notes. In: Proceedings of the international workshop on frontiers in handwriting recognition, La Baule, France
28. Liwicki M, Bunke H (2007) Combining on-line and off-line systems for handwriting recognition. In: Proceedings of the international conference on document analysis and recognition, Curitiba, Brazil, pp 372–376
29. Liwicki M, Bunke H, Pittman JA, Knerr S (2011) Combining diverse systems for handwritten text line recognition. Mach Vis Appl 22:39–51
30. Bertolami R, Uchida S, Zimmermann M, Bunke H (2007) Non-uniform slant correction for handwritten text line recognition. In: Proceedings of the international conference on document analysis and recognition, Curitiba, Brazil, vol 1, pp 18–22
31. Ney H, Steinbiss V, Haeb-Umbach R, Tran BH, Essen U (1994) An overview of the Philips research system for large-vocabulary continuous-speech recognition. Int J Pattern Recogn Artif Intell 8(1):33–70 (Special issue on speech recognition for different languages)
32. Rybach D, Gollan C, Heigold G, Hoffmeister B, Lööf J, Schlüter R, Ney H (2009) The RWTH Aachen University open source speech recognition system. In: Proceedings of the annual conference on international speech communication association, Brighton, UK
33. Dreuw P, Jonas S, Ney H (2008) White-space models for offline Arabic handwriting recognition. In: Proceedings of the international conference on pattern recognition, Tampa, USA
34. Dreuw P, Rybach D, Heigold G, Ney H (2011) RWTH OCR: A large vocabulary optical character recognition system for arabic scripts. In: Märgner V, El Abed H (eds) Guide to OCR for arabic scripts, Springer, London, UK, chap Part I: Development, in press
35. Dreuw P, Rybach D, Gollan C, Ney H (2009) Writer adaptive training and writing variant model refinement for offline arabic handwriting recognition. In: Proceedings of the international conference on document analysis and recognition, Barcelona, Spain, pp 21–25
36. Heigold G, Dreuw P, Hahn S, Schlüter R, Ney H (2010) Margin-based discriminative training for string recognition. IEEE J Selected Topics Signal Process—Statist Learn Meth Speech Lang Process 4(6):917–925
37. Dreuw P, Heigold G, Ney H (2011) Confidence and margin-based MMI/MPE discriminative training for offline handwriting recognition. Int J Doc Anal Recogn, In press
38. Gales MJF (1998) Maximum likelihood linear transformations for HMM-based speech recognition. Comput Speech Lang 12(2):75–98
39. Leggetter CJ, Woodland PC (1995) Maximum likelihood linear regression for speaker adaptation of continuous density hhidden Markov models. Comput Speech Lang 9:171–185
40. Dreuw P, Ney H (2010) The RWTH-OCR handwriting recognition system for Arabic handwriting. invited talk at DAAD Workshop III—On the way to the information society, Sousse, Tunisia
41. Christiani N, Shawe-Taylor J (2000) An introduction to support vector machines and other kernel-based learning methods. Cambridge University Press, Cambridge

42. Fischer A, Stahl V (1999) Database and online adaptation for improved speech recognition in car environments. In: Proceedings of the international conference on acoustics, speech, and signal processing, Phoenix, USA
43. Plötz T, Fink G (2002) Robust time-synchronous environmental adaptation for continuous speech recognition systems. In: Proceedings of the international conference on spoken language processing, Denver, USA, pp 1409–1412
44. Zhang ZP, Furu S, Ohtsuki K (2000) On-line incremental speaker adaptation with automatic speaker change detection. In: Proceedings of the international conference on acoustics, speech, and signal processing, Istanbul, Turkey
45. Caesar T, Gloger JM, Mandler E (1993) Preprocessing and feature extraction for a handwriting recognition system. In: Proceedings of the international conference on document analysis and recognition, Tsukuba Science City, Japan, pp 408–411
46. Kaltenmeier A, Caesar T, Gloger JM, Mandler E (1993) Sophisticated topology of hidden Markov models for cursive script recognition. In: Proceedings of the international conference on document analysis and recognition, Tsukuba Science City, Japan, pp 139–142
47. Schambach MP, Rottland J, Alary T (2008) How to convert a Latin handwriting recognition system to Arabic. In: Proceedings of the international conference on frontiers in handwriting recognition, Montréal, Canada
48. Schambach MP (2005) Fast script word recognition with very large vocabulary. In: Proceedings of the international conference on document analysis and recognition, Seoul, Korea, vol 1, pp 9–13
49. Märgner V, El-Abed H (2007) ICDAR 2007—Arabic handwriting recognition competition. In: Proceedings of the international conference on document analysis and recognition, Curitiba, Brazil
50. El-Hajj R, Likforman-Sulem L, Mokbel C (2005) Arabic handwriting recognition using base-line dependant features and hidden Markov modeling. In: Proceedings of the international conferene on document analysis and recognition, Seoul, Korea, vol 2, pp 893–897
51. Märgner V, El-Abed H (2005) ICDAR 2005—Arabic handwriting recognition competition. In: Proceedings of the international conference on document analysis and recognition, Seoul, Korea
52. Bianne-Bernard AL, Menasri F, Al-Hajj M, Mokbel C, Kermorvant C, Likforman-Sulem L (2011) Dynamic and contextual information in HMM modeling for handwritten word recognition. IEEE Trans Pattern Anal Mach Intell, In press
53. Al-Hajj Mohamad R, Likforman-Sulem L, Mokbel C (2009) Combining slanted-frame classifiers for improved HMM-based Arabic handwriting recognition. IEEE Trans Pattern Anal Mach Intell 31(7):1165–1177
54. Al-Hajj R, Mokbel C, Likforman-Sulem L (2007) Combination of HMM-based classifiers for recognition of Arabic handwritten words. In: Proceedings of the international conference on document analysis and recognition, Curitiba, Brazil, vol 2, pp 959–963
55. Vinciarelli A, Luettin J (2001) A new normalization technique for cursive handwritten words. Pattern Recogn Lett 22(9):1043–1050
56. Fink GA (2008) Markov models for pattern recognition—From theory to applications. Springer, Heidelberg
57. El-Hajj R, Likforman-Sulem L, Mokbel C (2009) Combining slanted-frame classifiers for improved HMM-based arabic handwriting recognition. IEEE Trans Pattern Anal Mach Intell 31(7):1165–1177
58. Plötz T, Thurau C, Fink GA (2008) Camera-based whiteboard reading: New approaches to a challenging task. In: Proceedings of the internaional conference on frontiers in handwriting recognition, Montreal, Canada, pp 385–390
59. Wienecke M, Fink GA, Sagerer G (2005) Toward automatic video-based whiteboard reading. Int J Doc Anal Recogn 7(2–3):188–200

60. Wienecke M, Fink GA, Sagerer G (2003) Towards automatic video-based whiteboard reading. In: Proceedings of the international conference on document analysis and recognition, IEEE, Edinburgh, Scotland, pp 87–91
61. Fink GA, Plötz T (2008) Developing pattern recognition systems based on Markov models: The ESMERALDA framework. Pattern Recogn Image Anal 18(2):207–215

Chapter 6
Discussion

Abstract In the last few years Markov models have been applied very successfully to the research field of handwriting recognition. In order to draw conclusions, in this chapter we will first summarize the state of the field, followed by the description of methodological trends and future challenges as they have been identified while analyzing the literature. Since the particular approaches as they were described in the literature are still difficult to compare *objectively* some general remarks on reporting results will be given additionally. The practical outcome of this final chapter is a set of guidelines and hints that should be considered for future research and development in the field.

Keywords State of the field · Trends · Benchmaking · Challenges

In the last few years Markov models have been applied very successfully to the research field of handwriting recognition. The first part of this book gave a comprehensive introduction into the theoretical and practical foundations of MM-based handwriting recognition. Furthermore, in the second part the general state of the research field has been surveyed.

In order to draw conclusions, in the following we will first summarize the state of the field, followed by the description of methodological trends and future challenges as they have been identified while analyzing the literature. Since the particular approaches as they were described in the literature are still difficult to compare *objectively* some general remarks on reporting results will be given additionally.

The practical outcome of this final chapter is a set of guidelines and hints that, at least in our minds, should be considered for future research and development in the field.

T. Plötz and G. A. Fink, *Markov Models for Handwriting Recognition*,
SpringerBriefs in Computer Science, DOI: 10.1007/978-1-4471-2188-6_6,
© Thomas Plötz 2011

6.1 General State of the Field

Tackling the problem of handwriting recognition does not necessarily require the application of Markovian models. In-fact, over the years virtually all major techniques from the wealth of pattern recognition methods have been applied to the task (including Neural Networks, Support Vector Machines, general Graphical Models etc.). Markov model based recognizers, however, gained special importance since they are apparently extremely suitable for the analysis of handwriting data. Today the field of Markov model based HWR can be considered being mature according to the large number of related publications and the existence of several competing recognition systems. This book gives an overview of the state-of-the-art in Markov model based handwriting recognition. Although certainly being highly desirable, a comparison of the general MM-based approach with other HWR techniques at that level of detail, which would be necessary for a truly objective judgment, is far beyond the scope of this book.

For online HWR the use of Markovian models is straightforward as the sensor data that shall be analyzed are sequential by definition and thus both HMMs and n-gram language models can be applied directly. For offline recognition the situation is different as images of handwriting—as they are processed in offline HWR—originally do not correspond to sequential data. In order to make Markovian models applicable to this kind of data, the images need to be serialized, which certainly is the most critical aspect of MM-based offline HWR approaches. Applying the sliding window technique is, basically, sort of a work-around that converts image data into sequences. However, there is no theoretical justification for this since humans do usually not perform something similar while reading (cf. [1]) and there is no physical image-formation mechanism behind. Nevertheless—it works very well in practice. By means of the "short-time" analysis underlying the sliding window procedure actual sequences of features are derived. This allows the use of Markovian models—the de-facto standard for the analysis of sequential data.

The superiority of Hidden Markov models for the analysis of sequential data lies in the fact that segmentation and classification are performed simultaneously in an integrated procedure. HMMs are able to cope with input data that varies substantially in length. On the other hand, there is not much motivation for applying HMMs to more or less static data with only little length variation. More precisely and being a bit provocative, there are better suited classification approaches in the field than HMMs for, e.g., isolated character recognition. As long as segmentation is not the most critical issue, HMMs might not necessarily outperform alternative classification approaches (cf. [2] for a general treatment of what "HMMs can / cannot do").

Similar to the majority of statistical pattern recognition approaches the theory of Markov models alone is not sufficient for setting up recognizers that can successfully be applied to practical tasks. There is always some sort of expertise within the particular application domain required to properly make necessary design decisions, e.g., regarding the choice of the basic modeling units, model topologies, model combination etc. (cf. [3, part II–Practice]).

6.2 Methodological Trends

When analyzing recent publications related to the field of Markov model based HWR certain methodological trends can be identified. In the following we will briefly describe the most important ones and discuss their impact on future research in the area.

6.2.1 Segmentation-Free Recognition

For online recognition handwriting data, i.e., x, y, (z) trajectories of the stylus used for writing can be fed into the Markovian framework "as is" since this kind of data is already sequential by definition. For offline MM-based HWR an additional preprocessing step needs to transform the originally two-dimensional data—namely images of cursive script that are recorded either using scanners or cameras—into a sequential representation. Although there are exceptions, today the standard approach for processing this kind of data is based on a transformation of the images into a sequential representation by the sliding window approach. Currently, practically all major offline MM-based HWR systems integrate modules that explicitly transform (word) images into one-dimensional sequential data prior to recognition.

Based on the sequential representation of handwriting data, the majority of current recognition systems performs segmentation free processing. Arguably, the segmentation-free paradigm for building the writing model can be considered the most successful approach to date for handwritten text recognition.

6.2.2 "Simple Structure: Lots of Parameters"

Similar to alternative application domains of hidden Markov models (cf. speech recognition tasks, or bioinformatics applications) model topologies of HMMs that are successfully applied for robust handwriting recognition tend to have simple structures. The majority of writing models is based on classical linear left-right (Roman) / right-left (Arabic) HMMs where every state is connected to itself (self-transition) and to its immediate neighbor in writing direction only. A slightly modified version—the Bakis architecture—also introduces skips of adjacent states. Apparently, complicated model architectures are used only very rarely. Instead of focusing on complex model architectures, researchers rather concentrate on the estimation of lots of parameters for output modeling. Most notably the multi-lingual HWR system by BBN consists of HMMs with simple Bakis topology but with (roughly estimated) 150k mixtures. The latter allows for very robust recognition of unconstrained handwriting.

6.2.3 Integration of Language Models

The use of language models is more and more becoming the standard for general handwriting recognition. In fact, five of the seven recognition systems reviewed in this book integrate language models for effectively restricting hypotheses of recognized sequences of characters or words that are generated by the particular writing models. Furthermore, it can be concluded that n-gram models represent the state-of-the-art for statistical language modeling. However, details about the language models actually used (method for smoothing probability estimates, perplexity achieved, integration with the writing model and so forth) are frequently not reported in the literature, which sometimes complicates comparability and potential adoption.

6.2.4 Use of Classifier Ensembles

The use of hybrid classification techniques for handwriting recognition has a rather long history. Various approaches have been proposed to integrate, for example, artificial neural networks and hidden Markov models into handwriting recognition frameworks. Recently this concept of combining multiple classifiers has been studied more extensively and it has been generalized with rather encouraging results. The integration of Markov models (both HMMs and n-gram models) into Ensemble classification approaches thus represents another recent methodological trend. Especially for the analysis of unconstrained handwriting with potentially numerous different writing styles or for huge vocabularies, parallelization to multiple diverse classifiers is promising.

6.2.5 Multi-Linguality/Script-Independency

Another recent trend clearly indicates the matureness that the research field of handwriting recognition meanwhile has reached. After more or less explicitly focusing on fundamental recognition problems (like, for example, how to treat two-dimensional data in offline recognition applications using statistical models that are, without substantial modification, suitable for 1-D data only), the community now has also turned towards other practical application problems like multi-linguality and script-independency. In fact, some of the reviewed systems have actually been used for the recognition of multiple different scripts and languages. The Siemens recognizer—originally developed for the recognition of Roman scripts—has been adapted to process Arabic handwriting, apparently requiring only minor modifications. The BBN recognizer has even been designed explicitly to cope with multiple languages and script types. The same holds for the RWTH system, which has been successfully applied to French, English, and Arabic handwriting recognition. Especially for a successful commercial application script-independency and multi-linguality can be considered very important properties of HWR systems.

6.2.6 Camera Based HWR

Offline handwriting recognition is usually performed on images of handwritten data that has been recorded by means of scanners. As one prominent example, for postal automation applications large, sophisticated scanning appliances have been installed in major logistics centers of postal companies aiming at optimal image quality. Recently, the general field of document analysis has been extended towards camera based input. The reason for this is the almost ubiquitous availability of cameras integrated into the latest generations of cell phone technology that allows spontaneous image capturing. Moreover, the emergence of new application domains like automatic whiteboard reading for smart conference rooms requires more flexible input devices than bulky scanners. In the last few years certain approaches for both online and offline HWR based on camera images have been proposed and have already been applied successfully. Although camera based input can not yet be considered an actual trend for offline handwriting recognition it corresponds, however, to a very promising and at the same time challenging application field.

6.2.7 Combination of Online and Offline Approaches

In the literature certain approaches have been described where either offline data has been rendered towards getting artificial online data or, vice versa, online data has been converted into offline. The goal of such techniques is to exploit the complementary information for the improvement of recognition. Whereas the first type of artificial rendering today is hardly used any more, recently offline techniques have been applied rather successfully for online recognition tasks [4]. One advantage of this procedure is that the problem of delayed strokes treatment, which in fact represents one of the major difficulties for online handwriting recognition, can be circumvented rather elegantly.

6.2.8 Universal Toolkits

Reconsidering the survey of handwriting recognition systems it can be concluded that most of those systems that are applied to practical tasks in both industrial and academic context are based on more general Markov model frameworks. Often these toolkits originally were developed for their use in alternative application domains—most prominently, e.g., for automatic speech recognition. When analyzing the general architecture of the systems, it becomes clear that the recognizers from BBN, IAM, TUDo, and—to some extent—RWTH are principally comparable. They follow— each more or less strictly—the classic approach of Markov-model based recognition for sequential data.

Many Markov-model based HWR systems are not publicly available including all the parameters and configurations necessary to set up handwriting recognizers from scratch. At least in some cases (Siemens, BBN) this might be reasoned by commercial interests. There are, however, publicly available HMM toolkits (HTK, ghmm, ESMERALDA, RWTH ASR etc.) that can freely be (and in-fact have been) used at least for automatic handwriting recognition purposes.

6.3 Some Remarks on Reporting Results

Ideally, other researchers should be able to reproduce results achieved by a proposed method. Therefore, when reporting results, besides the understandable desire to show the advantages of one's own method over others, it should be a primary goal to be as precise as necessary in documenting the parameters of the experiments. Such documentation comprises the data sets used as well as the parametrization and configuration of the recognizer. In the following we will discuss the problems related to these aspects and give some recommendations for producing "valuable" results.

6.3.1 Use Well Defined Benchmarks!

Comparability of results is only possible when working on data sets that are rather widely used in the research community. This almost immediately implies that this data either needs to be publicly available or at least available for reasonable costs. Unfortunately, the field of handwriting recognition is extremely diverse with respect to tasks considered—e.g., touching numerals versus handwritten text, Roman versus Chinese script. Therefore, there probably will never be the *universal* handwriting recognition benchmark. Within the different sub-disciplines one can, however, observe a tendency of researchers working on well defined and well known data sets—as, e.g., the results published for the recognition systems described in the previous chapter. Fortunately, fewer and fewer groups today still publish results on crudely defined or proprietary data.

However, a data set does not make a benchmark. For example the quite common practice to just subdivide the data "randomly" into training and test sets can't be reproduced by anybody and makes the largely optimistic assumption that the complexity and variability in the data is homogeneous. Therefore, fixed subdivisions into training, validation, and test data should be used [1] as they are sometimes already

---

[1] Though fixed subdivisions are good there is no reason to prove one's creativity by defining yet another one without giving clear reasons for it.

predefined for certain databases (cf., e.g., IAM-DB or the ICDAR competition configurations of IFN/Enit).

For a complete handwriting recognition benchmark now only the inventory of recognition units is missing. On the character level this might seem obviously defined. However, punctuation symbols and other special characters—just to give two examples—can augment a character set considerably and make a big difference in recognition accuracy. On the word level the problem becomes even more severe as it is not clearly defined what a "word" is supposed to be. For example "Mr." seems to rightfully be a word including the period. However, at the end of a sentence the final word and the punctuation symbol would clearly be considered separate units. This situation becomes more complicated if numerals and other special characters come into play. Obviously, these problems can be completely avoided on pre-segmented data. On IFN/ENIT, for example, it is sufficient to map the word image to the zip code of the corresponding Tunisian town. As, however, the real challenges lie beyond such tasks, it will be important for the definition of future benchmarks to address these problems properly.

6.3.2 Give All Necessary Technical Details!

Though the HMM technology constitutes a rather well defined modeling and recognition paradigm the devil is still in the details. Every reasonable HMM for HWR, which is worth reporting on, will contain quite a number of free parameters and configuration options that usually decide about either success or failure on a certain task. Therefore, it is absolutely necessary to report what basic type of HMM is used (discrete, semi-continuous/tied-mixture, or continuous mixture). For HMMs based on mixture densities it is furthermore important to tell whether the Gaussians used have full or only diagonal covariances (or use some even more sophisticated method of parameter tying). Additionally, the basic model topology (linear, Bakis, or hand-crafted), the type of elementary units (strokes, characters, or words), and the number of states used per unit are of fundamental importance. Though the algorithms for creating and decoding HMMs are pretty much standard it is better to also state explicitly how model parameters are estimated and how the model is decoded. The latter information is crucial as soon as a language model is incorporated into the overall recognition model.

For the language model part—which will most probably be an n-gram model—the type of smoothing applied (e.g., absolute discounting in combination with either backing-off or interpolation) and the perplexity achieved on the test set considered need to be given. Especially the model's perplexity is a crucial figure as without it there is absolutely no chance to either judge the achieved model quality or compare results reported on otherwise identical tasks but using different language models.

6.3.3 Use Hard Tasks!

It is a quite common misconception that high accuracy figures or close to zero error rates are good *per se* without considering the underlying task. There are two main problems with such figures. First, when operating in regions of ninety -nine-point-something accuracies an improvement in the second decimal is hardly statistically significant given the limited size of current databases. Therefore, improvements reported should always be checked for being significant at a level of at least 95%. All other minor changes in the results achieved are just noise and not worth reporting. The second and more severe problem of close to zero error rates is that any performance figure approaching its theoretical limit—i.e., 100% accuracy or 0% error rate—renders the underlying task useless. In such situations it is completely clear that the task considered has become too easy for the recognition methodology used. Therefore, as soon as improvements become marginal or even potentially impossible it is about time to move on to a more challenging experimental setup. The best thing to do to convince the reader that reporting on error rates ten times as high as in your previous publication is to make clear with a rigorous account of all details of the task addressed that you are really working on a hard and, therefore, interesting problem.

6.4 Future Challenges

For the automatic recognition of handwriting, the application of Markovian models has become a standard procedure. We identified several mature recognition systems that are being used for non-trivial recognition tasks in both industrial and academic contexts. According to the literature, quite diverse research directions are still being explored and standard procedures for building Markov-model based handwriting recognizers could not be established so far. However, some trends towards unified approaches can be identified as, for example, the quite widely used sliding-window approach for obtaining sequential representations from images of handwriting (offline recognition).

Although substantial progress has already been made towards the ultimate goal of automatic reading systems for handwritten script, challenging problems still need to be tackled. The most prominent one, which can be considered a universal problem of any area of statistical pattern recognition, is the problem of limited data. Though some notable data collection efforts exist and some quite substantial data sets have also been made publicly available already, these sample sets are still far too small—and probably will be for the foreseeable future—for training a statistical recognizer that might be able to show close to human performance in automatically reading handwritten script. Consequently, robust parameter estimation on limited sample sets remains an open research issue for MM-based handwriting recognizers. Extensions of classical model adaptation techniques or methods for discriminative training might provide the ingredients for solutions to this fundamental problem.

Major challenges can also be identified for the feature extraction process. Although the sliding-window technique has become a quasi-standard it has serious drawbacks, too. Most prominently, the dynamics of the process of handwriting is captured to a quite limited extent only. More importantly, however, there is no real biological justification for a small analysis window that is moved along the text-line as it is, e.g., for acoustic signal analysis in the speech recognition domain. From a theoretical point of view, holistic recognition approaches match the reading process performed by humans more appropriately. Current approaches are, however, not yet as effective as the classical sliding-window based techniques. Hence, further research on the convergence of methods is necessary.

Generally, the features as they are currently used for handwriting recognition applications are purely heuristic. In contrast to other domains there is no clear theory behind them, which justifies the feature representation used based on some underlying domain-specific knowledge about the signal data (the script images or the stylus trajectories) and its origin (handwriting performed by a human). Especially for more challenging recognition tasks aiming at the analysis of truly unconstrained handwriting with virtually no lexicon restrictions, further research needs to be devoted to alternative feature representations.

Finally, there is still only a limited overlap between methods applied to OCR and those used for handwriting recognition, which is understandable as OCR (as the easier problem) can be solved without putting the same effort into normalization, feature extraction, and modeling as is currently done in the handwriting recognition community. However, as demonstrated, for example, by the BBN and the RWTH recognizers a convergence of methods is quite promising. HWR systems could, for example, in the future also be trained on machine printed text and later only be adapted to handwritten data. The problem of limited data sets for handwritten script would then be largely alleviated.

References

1. Besner D, Humphreys GW (eds) (1991) Basic processes in reading: visual word recognition. Lawrence Earlbaum Associates, Hillsdale
2. Bilmes J (2004) What HMMs can't do: a graphical model perspective. In: Beyond HMM: workshop on statistical modeling approach for speech recognition, Kyoto, Japan, ATR invited paper and lecture
3. Fink GA (2008) Markov models for pattern recognition—from theory to applications. Springer, Heidelberg
4. Liwicki M, Bunke H (2007) Combining on-line and off-line systems for handwriting recognition. In: Proceedings of international conference on document analysis and recognition, Curitiba, Brazil, pp 372–376